THE NEW SEASONING

Graham Kerr

SIMON AND SCHUSTER · NEW YORK

Library of Congress Cataloging in Publication Data

Kerr, Graham.
The new seasoning.

1. Cookery.   2. Conversion.   3. Christian
life—1960–   I. Title.
TX715.K379   641.5   76–12480
ISBN 0–671–22172–8

ISBN 0-8007-0804-0 Fleming H. Revell Co.

To my wife Treena
who led me to Jesus

Dear Reader,

Well, so here we are again, back at the stove and the kitchen sink.

It's been a few years since my last book and I find myself in changed circumstances. In the late months of 1974 a profound change took place in our lives. My wife Treena "discovered" that she could love Jesus Christ and that He loves her.

In March 1975 I too became a Christian and from that moment He began to open my eyes to my life as a cook and as an author.

I could not write just a cookbook. I was (and am now) learning so much more about food that I have to share everything with you in this book.

No matter how well I thought I knew my subject as an "emotionalist" and as a "scientist," it all seems so insubstantial without knowing God.

Is it possible to use this book without knowing Jesus Christ as your Saviour and Lord? Yes, it's possible, but I must warn you that I have prayed most earnestly that these words may cause you to consider, if you have not already done so, asking Him to come into your heart as He has done with our family.

Having admitted this intent I can now relax and reveal to you some fabulous new thoughts for which I praise Him and give to Him all the glory and take for myself the just criticism where I have fallen into error.

Welcome aboard, friend—now let's cook!

His servant,

Rejoice Fellowship
Eagle, Colorado

Contents

SECTION ONE

PEOPLE
MAKE
FAMILIES

Good News!

What I'm going to bring to you in this book is all good news. There is nothing, not a single word, that spells doom or fear. I believe that we are living in a wonderfully blessed time and I just want to tell you why.

All of what I shall say is intensely personal; it has all happened to me and what has happened has completely changed my life and subsequently my attitude towards food. You have, substantially, in all areas—*one man's view*.

And now let me tell you about the really fabulous thing that's happened to me. It all began in late 1974, when things were really bad for us. Of course, looking at it from our new point of view, they were really *good for us!* But at the time things seemed bad.

My wife Treena and I had problems. We had problems with our family, with our daughter and our son. We had problems with finance —*everything* we had ever made from radio and television was suddenly lost in one fell swoop! Life looked utterly miserable, especially if you were as materialistic as I was.

Hoping to find some kind of help, Treena started a search. Anything that ended with an *ism* or an *ology* was something she looked at very carefully because it just might be THE answer to how awful we were feeling and how gloomy our marriage had become. At some point

The occasional footnotes are Bible references of which we had absolutely no awareness at the time that these events occurred. We have since that time been reading His Word constantly and have found these verses of great inspiration to our past, present, and future.

along the way Treena developed an interest in yoga. Following her lead I used to wind up with my right foot behind my neck, breathing in and out through my nostrils and letting out humming sounds trying to become contented!

Underlying all of this was the fact that Treena and I had shared for many years a mutual interest in the concept of reincarnation. The problem with reincarnation was that it was great over coffee but we had little time to consider Jesus Christ as anything other than a great teacher in His last incarnation. Seeing Him in this role we were unable to seek His love in faith.

The depths of the depression in our lives came just before Christmas of 1974. Treena, in sheer desperation, looked to God to provide the answer. She really didn't know what she was looking for. She had no idea at that time, since she had never read anything about the Baptism of the Holy Spirit.* She had no idea about water baptism. Well, she had no idea about anything! We didn't have a Bible in the house. We'd never read it and we had no friends who let us know they were Christians; neither had we any idea that anybody still wrote Christian books or recorded Christian messages on tape.

We were completely unaware of anything religious.

On December 17, 1974, Treena went to a little church in a village called Bethlehem In Maryland, quite close to our home, and in this church she was baptized with water, baptized with the Holy Spirit. She had a vision of Jesus, who spoke with her and touched her. She changed† absolutely from that moment on.

Treena decided that she should not risk "rushing the Lord" in any way, shape or form. She hid the process from me. She was praying every night to God to give her the direction she needed to help to bring me to the Lord. She was a *shining example*, without the Bible in one hand, without continuous conversation about the Lord, without going to church. She did nothing overt to bring me to the Lord. She left this to God.

One day, just before New Year's, I was in the supermarket, looking at the ever-escalating cost of meat, when the check-out girl came up to me and said, *"Isn't it wonderful. I was baptized in exactly the same way as your wife was."*

* Matthew 3:11.
† II Corinthians 5:17.

Well, of course, I didn't believe it, who could believe such a thing about Treena, with that awful temper, bad language and strong, stern desire to prove a point on the equality of women. After all, hadn't she been nominated twice for an Emmy award as the best producer of daytime television programs? Hadn't she produced nearly five hundred television shows that had gone all the way around the world? Hadn't she bossed a team of men just brilliantly and brought them all to the set every day filled with enthusiasm to make better and better television shows?

Treena was super blunt and gutsy, full of drive and self-assertiveness, qualities that seemed to me so far removed from the gentle kindness that spelled out the word "Christian."

I drove back home just full of the fun of it all. I was slapping my sides with mirth—this was the funniest thing I had heard in years!

I ran into the house, attracting all kinds of attention from the builders who were fixing the house at the time, and yelled out, "Hey, everyone, you've got to hear this!"

I told them of the conversation in the supermarket. *"Isn't it wonderful. I was baptized in exactly the same way as your wife was."*

Treena turned and looked at me and said, *"Well, it's true."*

Immediately, the whole thing fell in on me and with all these people watching, I turned around quickly and said, "Let's go talk about this."

Never during our ensuing discussion was there a suggestion that she thought that I needed to be saved.

"No, you don't need it," she said. "No, that's fine. I need it but I don't think you do."

That is submission.* Here was someone submitting to me when I really didn't know what I was talking about. It wasn't as if I knew the Lord—all I knew was Graham Kerr, who I thought was pretty good stuff, and I didn't need the help and guidance of the Lord.

Treena kept her peace and she kept her patience and she prayed every night and every day and every morning and every noon. She prayed constantly for her husband.

I had to go away and do some more television shows and we had agreed that Treena would not participate as producer. She had found that being at home with the children was much more rewarding

* I Peter 3:1.

than all the plaudits and all the backslapping; which had been almost her only motivation. I respected her view even though I needed her objectivity desperately. I now believe that God wanted us apart so that Treena could pray *and* fast as she did for seventeen of those days that I was away. I took a Bible with me and prayed each evening because I wanted to be like Treena but somehow I wasn't making it. Every time I prayed, I prayed right to the ceiling and that's exactly where it stayed! I had no idea what it meant to have conversational prayer—it was "God bless Mummy, God bless Daddy, God bless Auntie Flo" stuff. Then when I felt that there was something more to it, I would start saying the most extraordinary things to the Lord such as "Oh Heavenly Deity that dwelleth in the furthest extremities of the stars, beyond the outer reaches of man's vision, etc., etc., etc."! This I would follow immediately with an apology.

"Oh, I'm sorry, I really didn't mean that as it sounded," as though He didn't know what was going on in my heart.

One night after the worst possible day—the most difficult day of recording I think I ever have had on television in all these years*—it happened. After being on the set roughly fourteen hours, I returned to the hotel, showered and changed and was just going to fall into bed, thinking, "I just can't try again when I'm so tired." At that moment, it was just like a giant hand got hold of the scruff of my neck, walked me into the middle of the room, and dropped me on my knees.

Normally, I would prop myself up against the side of the bed for security.

I had the Bible in one hand and wondered what I was going to do. I said to myself, "*Boy, I really want this now. I want to be able to talk to God.*"

I think it was a burst of frustration at the contentment that Treena had—the peace and quietness that had replaced her rotten temper and that had made me understand that there was joy and peace and tranquility in this experience—and that I wanted it and wanted it badly.

I looked up into the junction of the ceiling and raised my arms . . . "Jesus, I love you." Quite simply, "Jesus, I love you."

It was like the whole ceiling disappeared, rolled back by the hand of God as Jesus reached down to me and loved *me* right back. I

* Matthew 11:28.

reached to Him and He reached to me; a wonderful thrill ran right through me. I chatted and chatted and chatted and chatted to Him about this and that and the other—we had our first talk together.

Praise Him and glory to Him. Wow! What a feeling!!

Since then, every evening and *every opportunity* to pray to Him is the *same opportunity,* this great personal contact.

Well, after that I just had to keep on working and doing and praying and asking my crew on the set whether they would mind not blaspheming as much as they did and they were just wonderful. They didn't scoff or jeer or laugh up their sleeves. They just went right ahead and stopped swearing.

When I returned home, after four weeks, I got to pray for the very first time with the woman I had fallen in love with at the age of eleven and with whom I had shared over half my life. I knelt with her and held the Bible in my left hand and her hand with my right. We knelt there and prayed *together* and that was the first time that we fused as one. The greatest physical and intellectual experience that man can have with woman, our mutual praying has never ceased.

And now, dear reader, here I am, a man who had been building a monument to the greater glory of Graham Kerr, a man who has now found out that there is someone much, much, much, much more important, and that is God. And through His son, Jesus, I now work for the greater glory of His love for everyone and because of this I find I am better at my work. It means a great deal more to me and there are no more frantic deadlines because He has made them *happy times* when I'm involved with people—His people.

Since *all* people are potentially His people I'm on safe ground when I tell you that I'm now writing *specifically for you* about a reformed way of cooking. God has been dealing with me on an *hourly* basis so that I may see clearly how He has changed my professional life and works.

Because His way is so wonderfully simple it follows that His concept of cooking is equally beautiful.

I have listened carefully and have interpreted His wishes into these words.

- Never be burdened by food preparation.
- Cook with a sense of responsibility.
- Feel love for those who are to eat your food.

ON BURDEN

Great cooks often claim a delight in their elaborate preparations and this may well be so, but I have found a certain heaviness in parts of the labor needed in the day-to-day feeding of my family. When the effort exceeds the reward, the activity becomes a burden and we regard cooking as "misuse of time." This sense of regret and dissatisfaction extends even to the good moments until it turns the whole barrel of apples rotten.

It is actually wiser to serve the simplest of foods—the fresher and more natural the better—than to attempt complicated culinary "tricks" aimed at improving your status as a cook at the cost of your freedom as an individual.

The "Great Cook" ends up by *performing* and sometimes loses that blessing that flows from giving with a generous heart.

ON RESPONSIBILITY

A home cook has two responsibilities. The foremost is to cook with a sense of responsibility for the correct nourishment of his/her family and friends.

The second is to use the available food budget to its best possible nutritional advantage.

ON LOVE

I firmly believe in "laying hands" upon the food *before* it is cooked and praying (yes, actually praying *every time*) that I may be continually reminded of my love for those who will eat the finished dishes.

And that is God's way of cooking for His people and I give Him all the Glory and all the Praise for His direction.

Personally,
I Don't Like to Cook

The "New Seasoning" is, in fact, a practical matter that costs nothing. It's simply a question of attitude.

Do you love the people you cook for, do you feel a responsibility for their health, do you like to share happy times, do you like to give of your own time *without* feeling that those you feed wind up in your debt?

If you do, then you've got the new seasoning and all I have to do is help you to use it.

If, by chance, you feel just a little reluctant about claiming the full list—then beautiful, let's share some of this honesty together before we get into the nuts and bolts of application.

Firstly, "I don't like to cook."

Wow, what an admission and it's only page 19 in what's now looking like a cook's confession!

Well, I don't and I don't think you do either! Let me explain.

I'd like you to decide upon a meal—write out your shopping list, go out and buy all the items, lug it all back home, unpack it, put it away, pull some of it out again, wash it, peel it, cut it, weigh it, cook it, watch it, strain or drain or skim it, cut or serve it, set a table and sit down to eat it *on your own.* Now get up, wash up, put it away, clean the kitchen and relax.

Did you *enjoy* that?

Did you notice the impact those three words had on you—"on your own"?

That's what makes cooking fun—it's sharing it with others, it is the simple act of giving that takes a backbreaking, often dull and repetitive task and turns it into a *joy*. It isn't the "joy of cooking"—it's the "joy of giving" that turns on the good cook.

Now there are some folks who really do love to sit down to a meal on their own. They fall into these broad groups:

Food Worshipers For these people the food is an end unto itself. It doesn't have to be shared because it started out as an exercise in self and why shouldn't it finish that way? You don't need an audience, you enjoy your own expertise and frankly—other people wouldn't appreciate it anyway. This is called, "Closed Circuit Cooking" and I simply cannot understand it—to my mind it's simply self-indulgence.

The Professional Slightly different from the Food Worshiper is the Professional. This person's life is spent creating and writing and demonstrating so that others who cook for families and friends may have suitable technical guidance. Quite often the timetable of a full day's work in the kitchen results in ample quantities of food being available at some very odd times. To just gulp down a spoonful and freeze the rest or just throw it out is a painful waste. The solitary professional therefore grows accustomed to eating alone to judge adequately what the results may be for you—the eventual cook. The *nature* of the game is unnatural!

The Single Person Whether because these people live alone, or because occasionally they get to be alone, it's rather the same. We all have this experience. Many people just give up and don't cook, they "snack along." A sandwich and a glass of milk with a good book. This kind of behavior is another kind of self-indulgence: you know you are hungry but you are on your own so you'll eat and think about *something else* whilst you eat.

Francis Hunter changed my view of all this a little while ago after we had attended a miracle meeting at which Charles and Francis had been ministering. She said, "But, Graham, I never have to eat alone. I share my meals with Jesus."

That really hit home. I thought of all those times that I'd eaten in a restaurant "on my own" and felt lonely and ill at ease. Now I could sit down and share the blessing with Jesus.

What a dinner companion!

. . . and what a help. A simple meal designed to protect and preserve His Temple, your body, against ill health or obesity, eaten sitting at a table—not crumpled up on a couch.

A meal to think about while eating.

Essentially, it seems to come down to the feeling that a meal shared with others is just fine, but a meal designed for one's own *self-indulgence* means that we are making a god of our appetite.

The new seasoning is the attitude of mind that prevails when you *know* that you love to give to others the fruits of your labors, because "to share" is what humanity is all about and the greater the effort, the greater is your gift.

The Reward
Equals the Effort!

In the home kitchen it is *so* apparent that just a little extra thought works real miracles, and when you think a little extra it means that you love a little extra.

Make no bones about it—the *seasoning of love* does make food better. That outgoing, flooding warmth for a child, or a husband, or a wife, or a cousin, or a brother—or a friend, or an unknown visitor. Love does mean a little extra care and a clean table. It doesn't mean *more* money or *more* volume or *more* cream—it just means *less* selfishness!

Let's look at the effort involved.

I'm going to assume that we are talking about two very different homemakers—both married with children, the husbands at the head of the families. The figures I'm going to use are my own estimates based upon a mass of conjecture and were not created to prove a point but rather to present a *conservative* comparison.

Mrs. Maria Troopington prefers to stay at home with her children, guiding and playing with them, and encouraging and helping her husband *to make do* with what "they" make as a team.

Ms. Dot Trumins is outgoing, contributes to the family budget by working and also contributes her skills for the general good of the community as well as to her family.

Maria has probably decided to be a full-time homemaker because of her upbringing. She might have been taught to cook, sew and tend a garden by her mother or grandmother. Many are these skills and they are close to the grass roots of our economy.

Maria faces the preparation of about 46,000 meals at the cost of about $152,940 and spends about 46,000 hours doing so.

Let us assume that at age 70, she has been *awake* for 409,080 hours; that means that she has spent approximately *11.2% of her waking life* preparing food!

Now for a look at Dot.

She didn't get much encouragement when she was young and never did seem to get involved in the kitchen. When she married at 20 she continued to work, except when she was in the last stages of pregnancy, and she was back at work, with a nurse or babysitter in charge, quite soon after her children were born.

She doesn't make breakfast during the week; the family get their own and it's often a stand-up-take-it-on-the-run affair. Even so, she would prepare about 17,000 meals at a cost of about $64,724—a higher cost per meal than Maria has because of her need for foods that cook faster and for more convenience foods.

Dot spends about 12,750 hours out of her total 409,080 waking hours or 3.1 percent in the kitchen.

Compare the two and it looks like this:

	MEALS COOKED	COST	TIME SPENT	% OF TOTAL WAKING LIFE
Maria (at home)	46,000	$152,940	46,000 hrs.	11.2%
Dot (working)	17,000	$ 64,724	12,750 hrs.	3.1%

It looks to me as though Dot converted 3 years and 9.3 months of "home cooking time" to "outside working time."

The big question, if you have been patient with me and followed (or even checked) these figures, is really directed at Maria:

"Is your extra 3.8 years of kitchen work really worth it?"

Human effort is usually measured in terms of worth by how much we earn an hour. If Maria received $2 per hour, we could change the question to *"Is your extra home cooking worth $66,500?"*

"Money's worth" means either happiness, contentment or satisfaction. Do we get this return for our "cash" investment and our extra years of effort?

The least we should expect is a sense of satisfaction: if we don't have that, *then something is wrong!*

The normal source of frustration—lack of this sense of satisfaction —is being ignored.

It's pretty rough, no matter how pure your attitude of giving may be, to cook up a storm and see it swallowed without thought or comment. I've jotted down some ideas on how to remedy this on pages 33–37.

Next on the list is being cheated by a packet!

It gets really awkward when someone dips his or her spoon into your instantly resuscitated powdered soup mix, tastes it and begins to *rave* about "your" cooking.

I have a friend who told me that a friend of hers had cooked a special cake each weekend for her husband for thirty years. He always praised her—in fact she couldn't wait to get to that oven because she loved to give and felt so rewarded by his compliments.

One day, she ran out of ingredients and used a cake mix lent by a neighbor.

That night her husband brought home friends. They all sat down to the cake and he said, "There—I told you, doesn't she make the best cake you ever tasted!"

That poor lady never baked a cake again. Completely pre-prepared packaged foods do help in reducing time and most folk simply cannot tell the difference but they *cannot* provide the essential creative satisfaction *we* as home cooks *must* have if we are to continue to cook for friends and family.

Another major source of dissatisfaction is in having an uncontrolled, unplanned food budget.

We absorb countless hours in profitless "worry" about,

"What are we going to eat tonight?" and

Must run up to the market for one loaf of bread," or

"Everything's getting so expensive I just don't know how to manage," or

"I'll get some multivitamin tablets just in case I'm missing something."

The one and only way to avoid *all* these daily worries is to PLAN, PLAN, and PLAN.

You only need a list of main dishes against each day of the week. Record how much you actually *need*, not how much is in the package at the meat counter. You can always shop for the meat first by simply pressing the bell and asking the meat man to pack you exactly what you need (see "Roast only what you need!" pages 119–20) while you shop for all the other items.

You can list the vegetables by type—i.e. green leaf, yellow or orange—then you can be flexible when you see what the market has that is really fresh and well-priced.

Finally then, add on simple desserts *if you must!* We sometimes consume homemade yoghurt (see page 212) with fresh chopped fruits, honey and wheat germ or granola—all delicious, fresh, easy to fix (and low in calories!).

A regular list of grocery staples such as butter, flour, milk, etc., should be literally printed out. You can then set against each item your *average* consumption. This provides a memory jogger.

Armed with a list you can then visit the market with *a known objective* and not for inspiration. You will have no doubts or worries anymore because you wrote it down.

These are just a few of the things that might help you to understand your predicament.

I say "predicament" because I know very few people who don't have some kind of burden in their efforts to run a modern home.

The fact is that our lives have been accelerated to such a degree that we find that even though we may strive to recapture the "good old days" by mastering the "good old ways," we eventually fail to be rewarded with happiness, contentment or satisfaction.

I have the feeling that quite often the Maria Troopingtons are missing out. They miss out because they see the Dot Truminses flash off in their cars to "work" and they, with a tinge of guilt, turn to their homes with like intent. But in Maria's striving for happiness, contentment and satisfaction, she seeks to "compete" with Dot by using her household *achievements*.

Quite soon Maria is burdened by a self-inflicted work load well in excess of Dot's combined effort at work and at home. She is unhappy, discontented and frustrated—and worse, she did it to herself.

Your husband, Maria, if I may call you that, didn't buy himself a slave; he married himself a woman whom he loved. Your husband doesn't get impressed by *good works,** he is moved by simple things done with love that happened because you had the time to think about *him* and not the Pâté en Brioche Flambé that needs to be kneaded every two hours.

The answer, Maria, is not in hard labor or in spectacular achieve-

* Luke 10: 38–42.

ments; the answer is to have the time to think and love and be loved in your own home.

You can start to do this *today* by seeking, in everything you attempt, *a natural simplicity, and seasoning it with love.*

For the Liberated Family

Judging by the statistics and the early morning talk shows, we have now come to understand that "Women's Liberation" is not just a term used by the few. It is a practical reality for many.

I do not want to get into the ifs and buts. I simply want to highlight one simple fact.

If the members of a family don't help to shoulder the daily homemaking responsibilities then either the working liberated woman becomes a *slave*—she has two full-time jobs—or the home runs down until it becomes a dormitory.

The only alternative is for the whole family to share in the several levels of homemaking. For example, children should make their beds and *clean* as well as tidy their own rooms. Meal preparations should be shared by every member of the family who is over fourteen. Certainly this means some urgent consideration to training. It does *not* mean that the family should just "do the dishes"—that simply isn't enough! Shopping should be shared, not simply errands; and at each trip a list must be made out (see pages 24–25), especially if the man of the house is doing the buying!

If all of this happens, then, in my opinion, the Liberated Family can well come closer together than ever before, and what some folk regard as a divisive threat to a happy, secure home can actually be a blessing.

But the secret, apart from simple willingness to participate, is in the twofold problem of organization and training.

The man, husband, father, "priest of the family," is the one who should set about the business of allocation. One of the greatest sorrows in either Christian or non-Christian homes is the dominant wife. Woman as wife is the weaker vessel (unless she's taken the Charles Atlas course and chosen to marry someone who should!). When she *submits* to her husband it puts the responsibility squarely upon his shoulders to dwell with her according to knowledge, "giving honor unto the wife, as unto the weaker vessel and as being heirs together of the grace of life."*

When Treena is in "subjection" to me I'm really on the spot. I must lead, I must protect and *I must do it right.*

All too often, in our Christ*less* past, when we faced certain domestic organizational problems, I would simply back off with, "Well, darling, you fix that, it's beyond me."

I simply wasn't a real husband to her. Gradually she absorbed the care of the "home front" whilst I went on to "wage war" on the business end of our lives.

The fact of the matter is, however, that where my family lived was the real "business end" of our lives because if that foundation isn't right it means you are *flying solo with your ego* and letting your wife run the airport!

All that results from that little habit is that you are always seeking permission to land!

So the husband must do the planning.

From experience I find that plans set up for domestic bliss *must* be flexible. That doesn't mean that they are compromised before they start. I just feel that, as they may call for some pretty major changes, they should be gone at gradually for a very short duration and then reviewed at a home meeting of the entire family.

The objective behind the reorganization should be to "Help Mother with the Home." I'm sure that a happy family always helps, but the crunch comes when Mother, for whatever reason, goes off to work. This is the time when everyone becomes a vital and valuable link in the family. A woman simply cannot do both functions without cheerful self-sacrifice from her loved ones.

Each family member can start out by offering his or her contribution toward cooperative living and toward easing Mother's burden. Notice the word Mother. Too often a son will offer to mow the grass, which is fine, except chances are that his mother never did mow the lawn in the first place!

* I Peter 3:7.

A brief rundown of what have become Mother's major tasks can provide a useful checklist for reorganization.

- Drycleaning delivery/collection
- Checking on medical and toilet requisites
- Cleaning the home, floors, drapes, dusting, washing windows, making beds
- Tidy-up time—plumping cushions, putting away games, papers, etc., carrying glasses back to the kitchen
- Making tea, coffee or cold drinks
- Making easy snack meals
- Writing up an order list for the supermarket and other stores
- Shopping, including unpacking and putting away
- Food preparation—washing, scrubbing, peeling, etc.
- Cooking, stove work, mixing and cutting
- Serving, "Can I do anything to help?" time
- Washing up and putting away
- Laundry—washing, ironing and mending clothes
- Children—supervised homework, P.T.A. meetings, doctors' checkups, special foods
- Correspondence—contact with relatives, schools, doctors, etc.

Now that you have read the list don't you feel that a woman who is a wife deserves a *real* family in her life?

So let the husband allocate according to an "offering" made by each member in order to "Help Mother as she helps us."

During this allocation time, Mother will probably start sounding off with all kinds of "guilt complexes." "Oh *no!* Really *no!* I can't have Johnny do the bathroom," or "Nobody knows how to handle that washing machine properly but me," or "It will cost a fortune to have Christine do the shopping."

To begin with, no doubt, all this is true; but then this is where the training comes in!

Simply divide up the list into skills and superskills. The skills can be explained within the family in the normal time available. The superskills have to be programmed for training.

Superskills such as writing a shopping list, shopping, cooking, laundry and child care can best be handled by sharing the experience. Older children especially can learn by actually using their hands under the Mother's guidance.

It is important to understand two things about these training periods. Firstly, our sex has no longer anything to do with the skill distribution. A boy can cook as well as a girl. There should be no reason why a boy should not be able to sew or wash or iron. In fact he *should* be led into some of these areas. If you feel this is strictly "woman's work," then please tell me how I, and millions of men like me, got on in the Armed Forces?!

Secondly, when the skills are mastered, the mother has a continual responsibility to offer constructive criticism and to compliment her new eager helpers. This is a delicate and wonderful opportunity for a "growing together" experience but it can be hopelessly lost if the work is haphazardly delegated without follow-up instruction, guidance, love and—above all—thanks.

I believe that work within the home should be rewarded by thanks and compliments and not with money. I believe that children's pocket money or allowance should be given *as such* and not as payment for "services rendered." There will be plenty of time for them to learn what it means to work for money and very few chances to experience what it means to work for love!*

I do feel that if the child does some special work for which an outsider would otherwise be used, then some additional payment could be made.

Finally, the man must be the earthly master. He must assume the responsibility for his family's successful living, because only in this way can the wife *feel* the full extent of her liberation; a liberation without restraint and without burden.

*Luke 12: 30–31.

Wow—Just Look at That Food, Lord!

Not so long ago we shared a meal with a truly wonderful man and his family who live quite close to Cape Kennedy in Florida.

Ed Gillespie is a Christian who is literally walking with the Lord. A man whose life and whose family's lives were in shambles until he gave it *all* up to God and God took it and worked one of His countless wonderful miracles. Today, Ed and *all* his family are Christians, loving and trusting in each other.

We had paid them a flying visit and had been invited to stay to dinner.

I should like you to know that, until I became a Christian, practically nobody invited us to share a meal; in fact we only ate at someone else's home about six times in twelve years! Since the Baptism, we have been going non-stop—Thank you, Jesus!

Now back to Ed and Gloria.

There wasn't much around to feed a crowd but a son-in-law started in on a heap of chicken pieces and before long a meal had been gathered up of backs and necks and salad and so forth.

I stood at the table ready to say grace—head down, hands clasped, eyes shut, ready and waiting for the "For what we are about to receive, etc."

Instead I got a nudge from Ed. I sneaked a peep at him—he was extending his hand. The rest of the family was holding hands in a circle round the table.

With eyes open and fixed firmly on the food, Ed spoke quietly and gently toward the table.

"Dear Lord Jesus, we'd just like to praise you and love you and thank you for this day and we would ask you to bless this food. Wow, Jesus, just look at that food—isn't that *wonderful*." He moved his head a little to one side, a great tender smile all over his face as he repeated so softly, "Wow—just look at that food, Lord! Thank you, Jesus."

I tell you that table lit up under his words. The Lord came down and Blessed that food *personally*. He sprinkled every piece with His seasoning.

Nothing—absolutely *nothing*—had ever tasted that good before. All the Savoys, Tour d'Argents and Pruniers of the world were suddenly faded by this simple meal in Florida.

And now it happens in our house and when we eat out as a family —I don't care where or with whom, because that kind of blessing really makes the food come alive for me.

There is no set pattern to our devotion at the table; we just give Him all our love and praise—ask to be forgiven for *all* those sins we have done since we last spoke to Him and then request His blessing on the food. We also add a few words asking Him to help us to help those less fortunate who may be without such food.

Our meals have been transformed by this easy, relaxed, informal and genuine expression of our love for Him.

I could pray for nothing more wonderful for you.

Conversation at Table

We had recognized the need to change the mood at our dining table some time before we began our walk with the Lord.

Mealtimes had become a battleground, an inquisition of the children conducted by the parents. It was a time of tension and rebuke, a laying down of laws, an opening of wounds into which the condiments were rubbed!

Such a situation is destructive to family life. At this last remaining tribal meeting place of our family-weakened civilization we must re-awaken a sense of sharing and joy. The dining table can be a place of joy, comfort, security—a place to gather new strength for the body and the soul.

When we garnished that meeting place with recrimination we got and deserved anarchy! Now, Praise the Lord, we have companion-ship and peace; we talk about joyful things. We try hard never to introduce a negative note or tone.

Let's look at what kind of pressure can be set up by even simple negatives.

We sit down to eat in the expectation of receiving certain "gifts." They are:

- *Regeneration*   Our body will mend itself.
- *Life*   We depend upon food.
- *Security*   We obtain peace and certainty of tomorrow.
- *Love*   We sense that someone *cares* for us.
- *Sharing*   We can discuss with our loved ones matters of mutual interest.

- *Relaxation*   We sit around in complete comfort.

If *expectation* becomes fact, then the family meals are a great joy and inspiration. If they are *not,* they can reap the following *disasters:*

- *Regeneration becomes Destruction*   The body under stress manufactures excess acidity; excess acidity eats into the digestive system causing ugly disturbances and complications.
- *Life becomes Death*   The tense, pressured, unhappy person tends to eat abnormally and compulsively. This can cause excessive as well as inadequate food intake. It is now known that in North America approximately one person dies every 41 seconds from FAD (Food Assisted Diseases). Much of this can be attributed to our *way of eating* and much of that is caused by our *speed of eating* and much of that is caused by our immediate family environment.
- *Security becomes Fear*   As a baby, we find safety and security at feeding time, but skip an hour and just see and *hear* the result! Those screams are a mixture of bewilderment and fear as well as hunger.

  Later in life we see the stove as a gleaming precipice supporting giant saucepans belching steam and DANGER, "Stay away from there, you'll hurt yourself. BURN, BURN, BURN—ouch—naughty!"

  Later on we are lifted into a highchair and given food from this danger area. If we don't eat it, we get, "Now eat up, just think of all those starving children in India. *Now you eat it up. It's good for you!!*" We grow up to fear our food times *unless* there is love and, through love, security.
- *Love becomes Hate*   Imagine that every time you went to seek pleasure you received an electric shock. Very soon you'd begin to distrust the so-called pleasure and avoid it. But when the pleasure is food then avoidance spells starvation, so you develop a *tolerance* for the shock. But that tolerance is only a coating that protects your hurt. When you come to family meals expecting love and you get criticism and anger, the coating is hate.

  This is a hard word for me to use and to accept, but I'm now telling you that the constant barrage of criticism we leveled at our children, at times when we should have loved and understood, caused them to *hate* us.

  Now we thank the Lord for turning that back into Love.

- *Sharing becomes Selfishness* All too often a child given a steady diet of confusion, criticism, overacidity, rush and fear begins to practice what we called in the army "dumb insolence"! He or she just sits there and refuses to communicate and as a result contributes, even more, to the strain and stress of the experience.
- *Relaxation becomes Tension* A really splendid chance to be at peace with one's children is lost and all the work and time and money and thought that went into the meal is absolutely and irrevocably lost—and in its losing we have planted a seed of potential destruction in those beautiful young gardens.

To ensure that mealtimes are times of warmth and sharing every family member must have a sense of love—of each other and of themselves.

Perhaps I can best express what I mean in a series of short letters to each member of the family who may join in the fullness of this family experience.

To the Mother:

Thank you for caring so much for your family and for your friends.

I know that you sometimes wonder if it is all worthwhile, those hours of apprehension over a new recipe or idea; only to be greeted with, *"Oh, it's OK, Mom."*

But we only truly fail when we don't try, and the burden of *retreating* from one's family is so much greater than that of caring for and loving them.

When you next get tired and dispirited look up the Gospel according to St. Matthew, Chapter 11, verses 28–30. It does wonders for me and I pray it may also speak to your heart.

To the Father:

This is an odd letter for me to write because whilst I have been placed, by the circumstance of being a Christian, back at the head of my family—I am still the part-time cook! Because of this I have a blended attitude as a man toward the food provided for my family.

Our food is there because God wants it there. The fact that I have worked hard does not cause God to reward me with the means to buy; He doesn't owe me anything because of my years of labor, my time in the Armed Forces, my "gifts" of income tax and social security, my tithes to the church.

We can be so hopelessly strapped to the physical need to provide and protect our family that our spiritual guidance as the earthly father tends to get overwhelmed.

I love the gospel according to St. Luke on this whole area; he gives me the peace to be a provider of His Word first, because by following His commandments and staying in fellowship with His people, we may never want for the *simple* things that maintain life. (Luke, Chapter 12, verses 29–32 says it *all* to me as a husband.)

As a cook may I simply add that there is a great need that your wife has of you. That need is a small, quiet word of thanks and praise when it is due, for the *work* she does day in and day out for *your* family.

To the Elder Children:

You are not alone. You have your family about you. Your mother cooks, your father provides—so that you can eat, live and grow up to have a family of your own.

When you were young you couldn't use your hands without endangering yourself, but *one* day you became mature enough to help.

When was that, when were you able to use your hands with skill?

There is a Psalm in the Bible that relates to this in a very special way; it's Psalm 81, verse 6. In this verse the writer is talking about Israel, but remove the word *his* and replace *her* and consider your mother as the object of this prophecy! What a wonderful feeling; just read it and see.

You see, it isn't only the manual dexterity that counts, it's the recognition that your parents work, in part, for *you* and out of *gratitude* you help them.

So please see what your parents do for you, help them and *be on time for meals.* There is no reason why your mother should become a short-order cook producing meals around the clock. It would be such a help if you were to adjust *your schedule* rather than add to *her burden.*

And when something tastes really good—a quick kiss and a hug for her, as an appreciation, will not turn you into a low-flying bat!

To the Younger Children:

Congratulations—you got off the baby food and now you have the biggest adventure you will ever have no matter how grown up you get, even more grownup than Mummy and Daddy!

Because right now you get to meet and eat all kinds of wonderful goodies. A lot of these will be new to you, so take a good look, ask Mummy or Daddy what it is, then sniff it and eat *just a little.*

Now *taste* it, let that tongue of yours *taste* it because your very own tongue can tell if something is sweet like a candy, sour like a lemon, salt like the seaside or bitter like a walnut.

There are so many wonders and it's such fun to explore everytime Mummy puts something new in front of you. It's a great adventure.

So eat up, it's exciting biting!

New Wine

One of the biggest and most interesting physical adjustments I have made since I became a Christian has been to "social drinking."

It's been interesting because of my historical association with it. I was brought up in the hotel business, the son of a hotel management team. When, at the age of twelve, I would talk to guests in the bar, I would have a ginger ale because it looked like the "real thing."

When I was sixteen, I helped out as a Wine Waiter and tasted (and hated) wine for the first time!

As I was surrounded always by very good wines and people who knew them, I was saddled with the *right* wines to drink. Wines that are *right* are usually *dry;* by dry is often meant arid and arid rhymes with 'orrid and that's how they tasted to me—like potent ink!

I grew to respect their status however, to understand that the taste of oak was a plus factor, that high tannin was a guide to a wine and would *eventually* taste good. I learned about sediment and sentiment, good years and bad years, soil content and grape varieties.

But the wine I liked best was soft, fragrant, white and with a full fruit "nose" (aroma). It was also rather anti-status, unless you lived in Germany or in Alsace Lorraine where this style of wine is made.

I never got a real taste for wine because I never got over the early social status wines. If I had been allowed to start sweet, perhaps then I could have "graduated" to dry.

My early years in the hotel business opened my eyes to some beautifully educated people who had delirium tremens (D.T.'s), a rather alarming condition in which a person sees little beastly animals and in a mixture of fear and repulsion starts to beat them off his person.

When you witness this in an exclusive cocktail bar filled with other "beautiful" people, and have to pacify the unfortunate, well . . . then you never have much of a desire to drink *hard* liquor.

I have never had a head for alcohol but I made myself join in because I used to feel *left out*. I was unable to *join in the full fun of a party* unless I had a couple. I always felt that I was being dull and a bore, since everyone else was laughing and chatting and I couldn't understand them—they were all bright, gay—a little loud, but . . . I I couldn't understand them.

I am now of the opinion that, after a certain degree of alcohol "they" couldn't even understand each other, that sentences are scrambled, words left out, continuity of thought is unimportant. They are *released* from their immediate environment.

So there I was, *always* painfully aware of being *left out* and finally getting physically sick if I joined in.

When we became a Christian family I did *not* suddenly give up drinking. There are no Biblical references that suggest total abstinence, though many that forbid drunkenness, but that we did not do—or did we?

The Concise Oxford Dictionary correlates *drunkenness* with *intoxication* and then explains that "intoxicate" means to "excite, exhilarate *beyond control*" (italics added).

The interesting point I make with myself about my social drinking behavior is, "When you used to drink in order not to feel *left out*, at what stage did you feel *part of*, and what do you think happened to permit this change of attitude?"

In search of an answer I wandered into the learned work, *Human Nutrition and Dietetics* by Davidson, Passmore and Brock.* They say, and I quote directly from Chapter 19:

> Alcohol. This drug depresses the higher nerve centres. Its *first* effect is to reduce the sense of worry and so to promote a feeling of well-being. It also loosens the imagination. Men and women come out of themselves, are more sociable and generally less intolerant of their fellow beings. For these reasons alcohol promotes good fellowship. If not abused, it is a valuable

* Stanley Davidson *et al.*, *Human Nutrition and Dietetics*, 5th ed. (Churchill Livingstone, 1972), p. 202.

social stimulant which has been appreciated by many civilized men.

I then reminded myself that the change that had taken place within me was a feeling of "well-being" that I had not previously had.

I *personally* saw this change as a lowering of my gift of discernment and accordingly my will to resist evil was weakened.

A Christian in a *weakened state* is clearly out of control or close to being beyond control and that means drunk, and this we are *forbidden to be*. And so now I don't go to parties where I feel *left out*. I either go to gatherings of fellow Christians and feel very much at home in the *joy of the Lord*, or I look around for someone to witness to. So if you see me at a party sometime, holding a ginger ale, move quickly or you'll get thirty minutes of great adventure that, if He wishes it, will turn down your imagination and tune in *reality*.

But, you see, people do get thirsty—so how exactly does one manage to provide drinks that are as compatible with food as wine used to be?

Well, you work at it, using all the admixtures of flavor and coming up with some wonderful homemade beverages. You will find some of our ideas for you on pages 218–19, but in using them *please* always remember this: Not to drink was *my* decision and in this book you are reading about my decisions about myself and how I feel.

One day, very early in our walk with the Lord, I stood at our bedside and spoke these exact words, "The true face of satan is the compromiser."

I am now, this day, confessing to you that I almost allowed my *self* to win on a matter that could have effectively compromised this book.

I have shared my views on the consumption of alcohol with you, but what of the use of alcohol in cooking?

My "second nature" has been telling me that wine is a vitally important seasoning. Its sheer aromatic power is justification alone for its use.

But!

What of the pressures created in the heart and mind of one who has been persuaded that alcohol is of the devil, and one needs little persuasion to see the devil's work in the manner in which this substance *can* be used.

What of this person who is torn, who is in two minds now that he or she reads of this *seasoning* in a book written for the express purpose of loving God?

Is this then a "Holy Invitation" to purchase and to handle a product that the purchaser would otherwise think of as like patting a wild dog?

I believe it is and I further believe that any use of any kind of alcoholic beverage by me in my work is an invitation to you to compromise.

Therefore I now renounce the use of any form of alcohol in my professional culinary life and in the name of Jesus I pray that all uses made of alcoholic beverages that I have recommended in either the "Galloping Gourmet" series or in "Take Kerr" or in any book, magazine or radio program, be now stricken from the minds of those who might otherwise be tempted to bring such substances into their homes under this culinary compromise.

I believe that the first step toward evil is the worst step and that every ounce of determination and effort is needed to rebuke it then.

Although this may now seem discursive, let me share with you my fear of flying—a fear so bad that I would study the weather a week before each flight!

I was delivered of this fear at an informal deliverance service. My faith that the demon was gone was mighty and I was once again at ease in the air.

Some time later, after several weeks on the ground I had to fly again and I looked at the clouds *out of habit.* As I looked I told myself that when I got into the plane all would be well; yet I permitted myself to take that *first* step toward the moment of fear.

You guessed it, I went up in the plane and the fear was back.

Now some folks will just say, "Oh my—the deliverance didn't work." But I know now that it isn't the focal point of the actual fear-producing experience that one must come against, it's guarding against the very first habitual step toward that fear that must be uppermost in our minds and *actions.*

So it is for the man or woman who has recognized alcohol as a fear or demon in his or her life. It isn't the temptation of the poured glass of sparkling wine set before you that you pray you can turn from.

NO! It's that act of habit in *passing* a liquor store, in *reading* a gourmet magazine, in *scanning* a wine list. In *reading* one of my recipes!

Now, Satan will use any of these devices to get you on his escalator, his moving highway that *always* leads downhill to that actual moment of temptation.

Because of this I'm not going to risk *your* or *my* utter joy in the Lord through a simple act of compromise.

In conclusion, with this whole matter of alcohol which this book has taught *me*, I must share with you a *personal*, repeat PERSONAL comment about wine in the Biblical sense.

I believe that the water that Jesus turned to wine, as His very first miracle, was a white wine, not the typical red wine we think of as communion wine. I believe that the wine was in fact unfermented. I believe it was unfermented grape juice because God would have never taken that first step toward evil in making from *water* a potent substance capable of being used by Satan.*

I believe that wine ferments when left at certain temperatures in contact with certain spores and molds that cause it to "work."

I believe that *this* is the working of the devil, causing these growths to turn the fruit of the vine into a forbidden fruit.

I believe that the mold is of the earth that God cursed: ". . . cursed *is* the ground for thy sake; in sorrow shalt thou eat *of* it all the days of thy life . . ."†

I believe that man found, in those hot and humid areas, that natural fermentation enabled him to *keep* wine that would otherwise spoil.

I am also aware that wine was better than water for the stomach's sake, since most of the water was polluted and dangerous to consume.

I am, and so are you, aware that today *grape juice* keeps well without alcohol, and that *water* is safe to drink, and that therefore the original need, born of necessity and maintained out of compromise, has developed into a gross dependency upon alcohol as a means to escape into unreality.

Therefore I believe Jesus turned water into unfermented, fresh, pure new wine.

We share with you some of our favorite recipes based upon this product on pages 218–19.

* "If alcoholic beverages were invented today they would be outlawed, just as this nation has outlawed marijuana, LSD and other dangerous drugs." (Dr. Dwight L. Wilbur, president of the American Medical Association)
† Genesis 3:17.

SECTION TWO

THE
SWITCHED-ON
KITCHEN

A New Priority List

Once you admit that the act of cooking can be dreary but the act of giving is such a joy, then all at once you feel like dashing into the kitchen and cooking up a storm for a whole crowd of folks. Well, that's fine but attitude isn't everything. Attitude needs direction—which way to go and how far.

To wrestle with this means to jot down a kind of priority list that sorts out the importance to you of the "influences" in a cook's life.

The influences are:
- Emotions (the senses)
- Nutrition
- Money (budget)
- Time (effort)

These are the main groups of influences and they can't be handled all at once. They must be considered in order of priority. Let me tell you why I've chosen to put them in the order I finally selected.

First, I have felt for many years that everyone put Nutrition *last*. If that weren't the case in North America then 50 percent of us wouldn't be overweight, 30 percent wouldn't be obese and we wouldn't be dying at the rate of one person every forty-one seconds from our FAD (Food Assisted Disease) diets.

I could see that Time (or effort) only looked like the first concern of most cooks because of all the "instant" products loaded on our supermarket shelves which promise freedom from labor. The mere mention of saving time causes many to forget that products designed for this purpose *must* cost more, *must* have fewer natural nutrients and MUST

45

taste less fresh and good. What a lot of negatives simply to gain a few minutes!

Budget and the Emotions have fallen somewhere in between Nutrition and Time according to how much money was available for the family in question.

All pretty confused and directionless.

So I went at it armed with loads of logic and this is what happened.

Emotions came first. By emotions I mean Aroma, Appearance, Taste and Texture—the senses come into play in that order. It occurred to me that if food didn't smell good, look good, taste good and have a good "feel," then a low cost, instantly created highly nutritious product wouldn't be worth a "tin of fish" because we wouldn't actually *like* it.

Nutrition came second. This was a much harder decision complicated by the fact that I've always related Nutrition to wrist-slapping dried-up old prunes who say sternly, "Don't eat that, it's bad for you," or "Eat this because it's good for you." Implicit in all this was a feeling that Nutrition meant Diet and Diet meant *suffering.*

Well, Praise the Lord, that's all over now. Nutrition is keeping the Lord's Temple (your body) in good working order, and the one thing that Jesus made abundantly clear in His teachings was that He suffered for us so that we wouldn't have to suffer (unless we *wanted* to!).

When once you grasp that nettle firmly, it takes as much weight off *your* mind as it will from your body, and boy, will you learn to eat well!

The big thing about Nutrition is that 90 percent of our chemical needs are all the same; but there is about 10 percent that is as different and individual to us as our fingerprints.

What a revelation! All of a sudden there is a reason for understanding about the 90 percent if only so that we can uncover our very own 10 percent.

The fact is that, at this time, we can not easily trade in our old misused organs for new spare parts. We assume that "all of us" is going to last all the way but if we abuse our bodies—we must be prepared for the consequences! Now can you honestly put that anywhere else but a close second?

Budget settled into third place. Pretty easy, this one, because only two influences were left—Money and Time. If you want to do things quickly then you pay extra for that privilege. The extra you pay for is *only* reduced effort since I am absolutely *convinced* that every instant product is inferior to the natural product it tries to replace and *always* costs more.

However, this doesn't mean that you must immediately throw out *all* those cardboard products. The sudden crush of labor and confusion would be impossible. What I recommend is that you go at them one at a time (see "How to Phase Out Cardboard Foods," page 74), master the replacement skill and move on. In this way you become the master of your own kitchen instead of a *resuscitation* device!

Time (or Effort) comes last. By putting the old winner in the losing position we get to win all kinds of races at once. We win by saving money, we win by getting a better supply of natural foods in a greater than "normal" variety, we win by having the food look better, smell better, taste better and having a better texture and we win most importantly by mastering new skills or relearning old ones. By practicing them we get the full joy of giving our very own labor and not the "packaged performance of others."

How do we apply these priorities?

May I suggest that you print up a card with these words:

AROMA
APPEARANCE
TASTE
TEXTURE
NUTRITION
BUDGET
TIME

Put it up in your kitchen and think about your food in that order—think about it when you plan your meals, when you go to the market, when you cut up and cook every item and when you serve and sit down to eat it.

Your food will improve, you will feel healthier, the food budget will either be smaller or you will buy much better foods, which will be glowingly apparent, and you will profit personally by turning effort into Joy.

"The heart of him that hath understanding seeketh knowledge: but the mouth of fools feedeth on foolishness. All the days of the afflicted are evil: but he that is of a merry heart *hath* a continual feast."*

* Proverbs 15:14–15.

The Emotions

There is no other human action that involves so many of these senses in so direct a fashion as eating.

We *look* at the dish, we *sniff* it, *taste* it, *feel* the texture and our digestion *feels* the impact later. Even our sense of hearing gets exercise from the sizzling sounds of a steak on a hot platter.

Since the emotions are our first filter, the essential step through which all our food decisions must pass, we should perhaps rest here awhile and consider them one at a time—rather than blindly agree that it should all be just . . . *nice!*

EMOTIONS (OR SENSES) IN GENERAL

Our senses are provided as testing probes that we extend from our inner selves into the outer world.

Essentially we can use them in a practical manner to determine what is safe to eat. Green mold on milk, a sour smell from a chicken, harsh bitter taste from an unknown berry, all are clear "back off" danger signals.

The same senses attract us to foods that are clean, sweet and nutritious. Have you ever considered how color relates to nutrition?

Can you name me one food (apart from some beans) that *looks* dull and washed out (overcooked) but has a high nutritive value? I can't.

To me color is a signal of nourishment. *Provided* that the color is bright, natural and typical of that food—it *must* contain more "goodness."

At the same time our concern with sensual pleasure can get out of hand. The problem is substantially one of indulgence. To indulge one's senses seems to me like recognizing that they exist. But don't let the senses rule you. You are designed to rule the senses. Let them *serve* you. This means by using them we get to be critical of what we consume.

When this critical judgment is exercised meal after meal we begin to reject greasy french fries, grey-green tasteless beans and limp salads.

But there comes a time, and it is so hard to know the exact borderline, when the indulgence becomes overindulgence.

Like all our "testing" probes, their over-use rubs the senses raw with emotion and habit or dependency starts to develop.

I think it's important to magnify that word *dependency*. When we become dependent we are actually losing control of the situation.

How many times have you heard a rather overweight person say, "Giving up sugar in my coffee is easy but I never seem to remember— it's second nature to add it."

Second nature is exactly what it is, repetitive function; your own fresh sensitivity and control is your first nature, given to you by God. Now God is so generous that he gives us the complete freedom of choice. We can go along with God's First Nature or we can, through habit, run the risk of handing ourselves over to Satan's second nature.

Isn't God wonderful to give us that freedom of choice?

It's because of this that I'm now a strictly First Nature Cook and I'm always on the lookout for those second nature compromises that lead one into overindulgence.

Overindulgence comes when you start to notice a habit forming that disturbs you.

I have a wonderful warm friend who, when he is away from home, sneaks into ice cream parlors for a vast spooning of multi-flavors. He adores it, and freely admits that he's at least fifty pounds overweight but argues that "It's a pretty small vice for a big guy like me!"

The fact is that he's hooked on an overindulgence, *it's second nature to him now*. He has lost control.

I have labored this point for a very important reason. There is a chance that, in the notes I'm about to make, you will find some ideas that could literally turn you on to *your* food to such an extent that you may be hooked on your senses.

Remember you have your senses and you should harness them as an exercise in avoiding what is bad or of poor quality but when a specific food becomes a habit that concerns you—*watch it!*

THE AROMA-ZONE (*Smell*)

Our sense of smell is the absolute first, foremost and most fascinating of all the senses.

Aroma is the first thing we perceive on entering a house, no matter how well ventilated!

It is the smell of freshly baked bread that helps to make a house smell like a home.

It is the smell that really stimulates the tastebuds. Try holding your nose (the way you would when swallowing medicine) and see how greatly reduced is your sense of *taste*.

Aroma, then, is the cook's foremost concern. Try to surround the people you feed with a "cloud of aroma." Here are some ideas to heighten the pleasurable sense of smell:

- Hot food must always be *hot*. So must the plates and the covered serving dish. It is important to cover or enclose the food so that when you raise the lid all Heaven breaks loose! Remember hot air rises and with it go the aroma molecules.
- The aroma content depends upon the release of *volatile oils*. These oils are found in huge quantity in garlic, shallots, and onions; their structure is completely different in each case. Still more complex oils come from herbs and spices and citrus fruit skins. It is their aroma *when heated* that you are looking for; so sniff first, then add, then sniff again. This way you get to "exercise" your sense of smell and learn what works where and how much.

Be aware of intruding aromas that are *not* in the list of ingredients —such as:

- Strong-smelling perfumes, after-shave lotions and hairdressing oils. All of these can really disrupt a well-executed dish.
- Strong-smelling flowers such as gardenias and some roses. These have no place on a dining table.
- Furniture waxes with artificial lavender or lemon overtones.
- Perfumed bathroom soaps (especially in certain well-meaning restaurants).
- Heating fuels, such as methylated spirits used in table lamps.

Try to visualize a "pyramid of aroma" with its base covering your plate and the apex at your nose. This, dear reader and fellow cook, is our area of responsibility—we must fill this aroma-zone with flavor.

THOSE THOUSAND AND ONE TASTEBUDS (Taste)

God created all of us more or less equal with about one thousand tastebuds. These curious little fellows are "odd organs." Odd inasmuch as they are totally different from any other "organ." Generally their cells do not divide. They contain no blood, they have no lymphatic glands. They appear to be *nourished* by a protein found in the saliva and the "nature" of this protein pretty well determines the quality of our ability to taste.

Add to this a natural erosion and you may wind up with about three hundred taste buds of dubious function.

The bud itself appears to be set up to receive information of at least four qualities:

- *Sweet* This is the strongest receiver—comes on first but doesn't hold for long. Predominant in both the young and elderly.
- *Sour* Combines very well with the sweet because it lasts longer and gives a decided double "impression."
- *Salt* Very much "desired."
- *Bitter* Develops in adulthood but fades in older age.

So all you need to know about the workings of these four basic qualities is

—that the sweet sensation is uppermost but leaves early in order to make way for any of the others.

—that sour is the best companion to sweet because it provides a refreshing aftertaste.

—that salt invigorates the bud, but be careful here that you don't overdo it—we only need roughly ¼ teaspoonful of sodium per day.

—that bitter is the longest-lasting sensation and the least dependency inducing. It generally satiates the appetite such as is the case with Belgian endive salad.

The main taste objective is to establish the central character. If this is chicken, then let the chicken *taste* be encouraged by lesser, compatible tastes. Obviously sweetness will mask the natural taste if overdone. A little honey blended with lemon juice can quicken the interest like a fanfare of trumpets announcing the arrival of a king (in this case the chicken!).

Always *add* with a light hand, then taste, then add again. *Nobody* can ever know enough to add and never taste. In fact, if you don't taste a sauce or seasoning before you serve it, you are, in my opinion, doing what you do without love! I know that diet-watching organizations forbid tasting, but I'm referring to the *final* taste or correcting the seasoning. This *must* be done or *all* your effort can be a total waste.

There are other taste dimensions, one of which has been recognized by the Chinese and Japanese for centuries. This dimension is the full, round flavor of fats and oils, substances that abound in our Western diets. Because it is the fats in meat that add the rich flavor, the Japanese became aware that those people who ate little fat meat—or none, like the Zen Buddhists—lacked this rich-tasting flavor in their diet. To make up for this deficiency they developed soy sauce made from soy beans, wheat, water, salt and a special yeast culture. This provided an alternative to the animal fat so abundant in Western diets, the same fat that *appears* to represent such a threat to *our* health.

If we reverse the roles and remove the fat from our food and add a little of their soy sauce we achieve a valuable health goal and we *replace without suffering.*

Inspired by the "taste alternative" offered by this substitution, look for means by which we can reduce sugar, salt, and fat content. Take out the empty calories and replace them with a mouthful of flavor—this is the great new challenge for the twentieth-century cook; a blend of science and emotion, a better taste *without* suffering a body insult!

TO SUIT THE TOOTH (Touch)

Our sense of touch comes into play at the same time as taste. It is less important when a taste is good but more important when it is poor.

Let's look at this!

A well-seasoned, tender, yet "crisp" steak can be appreciated for its flavor, providing the texture is smooth and "melts in the mouth." We tend at that time to recognize the stronger sense of taste.

On the other hand a tough steak may have *more* flavor, as with *some* of the grass-fed cattle, and yet so occupy our sense of touch that it *overrides* the taste.

Quite often we spoil the texture simply by overcooking.

Most meat protein contains almost 70 percent moisture—the retention of which should be the aim of the switched-on cook.

Most surface moisture can be lost by too high a temperature. When the surface exceeds 212° F. (boiling point), then you get evaporation. Since the tissue is only 30 percent of the total, it follows that with any major loss of moisture these fibers will collapse upon themselves and shrink. Shrinkage in meat is therefore a visual clue of dryness or excessive temperature.

In addition to this moisture loss you have the *really negative* reaction on connective tissue. Cheaper cuts have more of these strips of gelatinous connectives that enclose, support or "tie together" the major muscles. The more work a muscle has to do the more concentrated are the connective tissues. Because of this we pay *less* for such cuts.

If these cuts are cooked at too high a heat, the connective tissues simply tighten like a spring and literally *squeeze* the moisture from the meat, quite apart from becoming, in themselves, as tough as boot leather!

The whole secret to *touch* is therefore in the selection of the best degree of heat coupled with the right amount of time to do the job.

I'm inclined to think that this means the longest time at the lowest safe temperature. The safety factor involves bacteria because meat must be heated above 140° F. in order to prevent the incubation of staphylococci bacteria. The long-long-slow-slow cookers and ovens that switch themselves on and off present real problems in this general area.

All the temperatures used in this book are selected with this "balance" in mind.

ONE LUMP OR TWO? (Smoothness)

Apart from tough protein, I must say that sauces, custards, cream soups and toppings are all subject to lumps. Nothing, in my opinion, pinpoints the careless (without love) cook more than the stray lemon pip, the poorly blended sauce with its specks of flour "dumplings," the tomato seed or wrinkled skin. All can be avoided with a simple fine mesh strainer. Some cooks (such as myself in the past) excuse the lumpiness of their dishes by saying they are "peasant style." A revolting put-down to our fellow man.

Add to the lumps—the grit. One plateful of gritty, sandy spinach or leeks or Romaine lettuce is enough to convince anyone that the cook was thinking of something else at the time!

DIGESTION

I call this the "sixth sense." It isn't discussed too often in cookbooks, yet it does more to spoil an apparently "perfect" evening than any other single fault.

Indigestion is your body's way of "screaming" with pain.

The usual way to combat this extreme discomfort is to take an antacid pill or tablet, powder or potion.

I will not tolerate any such product in my digestive system.

If I eat at high speed, eat on the move, eat without thinking about the food, eat whilst having a business discussion, eat on the wrong "clock" when flying around the world, eat too much fat, too few crisp vegetables—any of these common errors—I will get indigestion.

I sit there and take it in the belly. I will groan, squirm and pant with the pain (you know what *men* are!) but I will *not* kill the pain.

My body is screaming, "Don't do this to me." So I sit there and work out exactly what I did to it and I promise *never* to do it again.

Since one bad night in Frankfurt I have, praise the Lord, avoided such disorders. The Lord's temple is no place for such an outcry.

Better *is* a dinner of herbs where love is, than a stalled ox and hatred therewith.*

CAUTION!

Indigestion may arise from a variety of sources—not just sauces!

Be sure that *yours* never returns by taking the initiative and avoiding the foods that pain you. If the pain persists however, then you must get together with your family physician and discuss the matter.

And while on this point of medical attention, I should like to share with you our family attitude to Jesus as healer. We *always* ask Jesus first to heal us, then we take our sickness to a human professional—*without delay*—and we continue to pray. We believe that Jesus will work His own miracles in His own way and in His own time and this may include passing His power through *your* physician.

This is why we lift up our health to our Saviour and then act in concert with Him in faith with a physician.

I simply do not believe that the Lord Jesus passes His *healing* through an antacid tablet that permits those who consume them to continue to overindulge.

* Proverbs 15:17.

How the Other Half Dies

At this very moment, spread thickly over the poorer nations of the world, four hundred million human beings are slowly, inch by inch, starving to death.

I knew this before I became a committed Christian and I was often quoting statistics at people, largely, I think, because my conscience bothered me.

How could I cook like that? I was a butter smotherer, a fat fryer, a super stuffer of mankind. No wonder Weight Watchers voted me Public Enemy No. 1!

I would defend my public position with extraordinary double talk by professing concern for my fellow man and exhorting my fellow food stuffers to eat less and give more.

I would go directly from such broadcasts to luncheons and dinners and promptly fail to practice what I had preached. At home our waste element was awful, our concern for the starving was far from our minds.

My charity *stopped* at home!

Then Jesus came into that home and tears fell from my eyes at the thought of this same problem.

We attacked our food budget, reducing it by $700 a year. We gave $350 to a major relief organization and used the other $350 to improve the nutrient aspect of our food by buying fewer *empty* calories and investing in more natural food elements.

To waste food is a crime in our home, a crime against our fellow man. Our feelings *start* in our kitchen and lest any man scoff and say, "What good will that do for an African woman and her child?" I'll tell you.

When one man loves another man and denies himself for that man, then God looks after the complex machinery of redistribution.

Just see how he would do it in our nation today. If we *all* declared war on our own personal waste of edible foodstuff we would have the potential to save four billion dollars' worth of food.

If we *all* denied *ourselves* for our fellow man *we* would want to see that our Government gave directly to those human beings.

Do we do this now? I don't really believe so.

Certainly we give, but do we *sacrifice?* Giving isn't enough. We can't give and then consume 1,603 calories by eating a sixteen-ounce porterhouse steak. We can't give and then keep (as we did) a 110-pound dog who did nothing else but eat. We can't give and maintain a surplus fat covering on our body at 3,800 calories a pound, when that one pound of fat would give life to three men for a day.

I consider myself superblessed by God because I live right here in the United States and I've been superblessed by God through living in Britain, New Zealand, Australia and Canada—all places where the land flows with "milk and honey," enough to eat—starvation unnecessary.

Yet I've seen millions of undernourished, sick and diseased people who, we are told, die at the rate of one every three quarters of one second due to a lack of food. That's as fast as you can click your fingers —go on, try it, it will make you sick to your stomach over your last meal if you ate it with indifference and without thanks.

Today 10,000 fellow human beings will die from a food-assisted disease whilst we affluent dwellers in the promised land are also dying from a reported *over*consumption at the rate of one every forty-one seconds (estimated 768,750 per year—see pages 59–60).

One major Life Assurance Company advises that statistically, if I'm 25 percent above my correct weight at the age of forty then my life expectancy is reduced by that same 25 percent!

That means that if I store up excess food upon my body while another dies for a lack of food, then I'm guilty and I shall be punished even unto death!

As a result of our changed attitude, our home of excess has now come back to the right weight and when we eat, we eat for our specific body needs.

Part of this discipline is to get to *know* exactly what we need in order to correctly maintain our health.

All human beings are roughly 90 percent identical to one another in the way we receive and use food. It is the other 10 percent or so that is as different and individual as our fingerprints. This percentage can vary from 5 to 20 depending upon the individual. What is important is that we get to know our own *percentage.*

It is this percentage that *could* cause us to develop gout or rickets, diabetes or heart problems, kidney or liver malfunctions, limit our brain cells or raise cholesterol, and it almost certainly makes some of us obese and dyspeptic. The list is *potentially* endless.

It is, of course, far too pat an answer to say that an adjustment in your food intake can cure all of these medical problems. It is equally misleading to fail to recognize that heredity and cultural influences also bear heavily upon all of them.

At the same time, however, it is undoubtedly true that a great many of our bodily malfunctions could be partially prevented or arrested by *knowing* how to adjust the daily fuel for our *particular* engine.

Before we get into how this is possible, let me share with you why I feel so strongly about the need for this knowledge.

In the Bible we have this clear statement: "Know ye not that ye are the Temple of God and *that* the Spirit of God dwelleth in you? . . . If any man defile the Temple of God, him shall God destroy: for the Temple of God is holy, which *temple* ye are."*

Imagine . . . I am the Lord's Temple—and if I fill it with all kinds of junk and cause it to malfunction as a result, *then I defile His temple!*

Well, O.K.—so how do we set about knowing our own percentage?

Firstly, we must decide that our responsibility as home cooks is to *all* those we feed. That our children cannot be expected to know as much as we *should* know, that they rely upon us to provide for their health and vitality, both now and in the future. Ours is an enormous responsibility but it isn't a crushing one—it's exhilarating, and gives real *purpose* to what was (or might have been) hitherto a rather dull, repetitive and boring business.

So we must know the family's percentage.

This requires an annual blood and urine analysis and this *used* to be expensive.

I say *used* to be because while everything keeps on going up, medical science has been able to provide central facilities that have replaced the old Bunsen burner and test tube tests with a computer readout that covers sixteen different subjects *for the price of two* (about $15).

* I Corinthians 4:16–17.

Of course you can dismiss all this and cook along by instinct. You can easily convince yourself that *you* know what your family needs are and you certainly don't want a computer to threaten *your* daily menus by introducing smart little figures that give you something else to worry about in addition to inflation, etc.

After all, they all look fit and healthy, no cold or flu and you zap them with a multi-vitamin to take care of any oversights!

Well, that's up to you; as I said earlier, it's simply a question of degree in your own developed sense of responsibility to your family.

Food-Assisted Disease

I get so concerned about statistics and their place in our lives. We praise those that prove *our* position, decry those that don't and falsify the rest!

Of one thing however, I am sure—we do die.

We also die of a potentially endless series of minor or major malfunctions.

A large number of these malfunctions are caused by the air we breathe, the liquids we drink and the food we eat.

Nobody has, as yet, done a thoroughly scientific study of the root cause of deaths by percentage. That is to say that there are no *absolute* figures to indicate the deaths due to *incorrect* eating.

We do know, however, the number who died in the United States from diseases that are assisted by incorrect food consumption (usually overconsumption of substances with adverse body impact).

These somber statistics are gathered by the National Center for Health Statistics, Washington D.C., and are published each year with a three- to four-year delay.

The latest figures* show that 46,000 people died of glandular and nutritional diseases. Of the 5,000 who died of blood disorders, almost 3,000 could be set at diet's door.

Four thousand went with alcohol-induced mental disorders. Another 23,000 died from blood pressure and other malfunctions of the circulatory system.

Six hundred sixty-six thousand heart attacks were fatal. There were

* 1970 at time of writing.

207,000 strokes. Of these two we may only question the number that could have been avoided or delayed by better diets—no figures yet exist that can provide these facts. *Conjecture* places the avoidable as high as 75 percent.

Thirty-two thousand had faulty arteries; 23,000 died of respiratory diseases complicated by excessive weight. Eleven thousand people experienced and died of cirrhosis of the liver—alcohol again!—while another 9,000 developed fatal digestive-system diseases. Another 1,000 died from urinary system defects.

If you add these deaths with others that have a direct or probable relationship to malnutrition (bad nutrition) you get 768,750 in one year in one nation.

That places one death each forty-one seconds at the kitchen door.

We have it within our power to come against these deaths where blind excess is involved.

We can claim a healing through compassion. A healing given us by a God who sees that we, as a nation, have concern for our fellow man, for the man that now dies each three-quarters of one second from food assisted diseases caused by *under*eating.

Let us give of our excess so that a life may be saved . . . *today.*

God's Plan for
the Overweight

In all my other chapters Jesus comes to you as a kind of "love" factor that, if accepted into your heart, would transform the very fibers of your food because He will have changed your attitude to those for whom you cook.

I present him to you in this manner because I went forty years in a wilderness without Him and when I was awakened to Him, it was not because anybody was forcing Jesus on me. In the past I didn't know what was lacking. I seemed to manage.

What was missing was the glow of thanks to Him for His blessing, for His raw materials and for His generosity in singling out my little family to love. Now with constant love and praise to Him, my ability as a cook has just forged ahead as though I had had the brakes on for years. Now I can see it as God's plan and not *mine!*

But when it comes to "God's Plan for the Overweight," I am dealing with a condition that, *in many cases,* needs a healing miracle. Not a miracle that suddenly causes you to lose fifty pounds and snap back to what you feel you should be, but one in which your attitude toward yourself changes and the pounds melt away *forever.*

As before, dear reader, I do have some non-Christian advice for you. It will work and it will be a struggle and like all other such weight-loss routines I must tell you that the pounds are likely to return, no matter how skilled and knowing the advice might or might not be.

On the other hand I *believe* that you can hand the whole problem to God, and since I believe in the proper channels of communication, I

* See note on page 70.

61

would recommend you do this through Jesus, His Son with whom you can be sure that you can have a person-to-person relationship over your healing.

I believe that Jesus can heal you if you are badly overweight; thus the views in this chapter are not like those in other chapters where I stress my Christianity as *intensely personal* and my feelings about Jesus as relating to my own life and what He has done for me. In this case I'm telling you that I believe that He can help you.

Since this can be viewed as a "quack faddish" idea and reflect upon me as a "quack faddist," let me quickly say to those who will *have* to judge me that, in the paragraph below, for the word "reward," you can use the words "Salvation" and "Love."

Weight Watchers use a costume pin and citations as prizes for weight lost and maintained. *Slim Chance in a Fat World* uses *tokens* that you can exchange for a new dress or fifteen minutes' extra chat with your husband (I don't know what men do).

Reward is the key to *all* these "diets" or "reforms" and when you believe in God, and when you go to Him with a problem, you get your *reward* instantly—you get *love*. That's it, not a reward in six months or a year when the correct clothes size is yours again but right now, a genuine awareness that I AM LOVED RIGHT NOW, JUST AS I AM—HE LOVES *ME*.

And that's just for openers!

I believe with all my heart, with all my soul—and the Holy Spirit is just sloshing around this clay vessel as I tell you this—I *know* He can help you, help you right now. If you haven't accepted Him, accept Him now, just kneel down, *wherever* you are and raise up your arms *wherever* you are and say out loud *wherever* you are—"Lord Jesus, please come into my heart, please help me, I surrender myself to you completely."

Then be quiet and listen and allow yourself to feel. He has the fastest *right* in the Universe. Like a flash He will reach down and let you know He is with you. This experience is different for everyone, so just relax (which I suppose depends on where you are!) and you will be blessed with a sensation all your very own.

Now you can get up and get on with those pounds you want to lose because He has touched you, the miracle has been done, He lives within you now as your companion, guidance system and personal *nutritionalist!*

What a blessing it is to have Him as a twenty-four-hour-a-day advisor.

Isn't it better to go back to the maker if you have a defect? If I had been made by Yale or Harvard Medical School, I'd go back there with my extra pounds and say, "Look, something seems to be amiss, would you please fix it."

And in my case, all they would say would be, "Sure, just eat five hundred calories a day less and it will be gone in sixty days."

And that would be all I would need to do *because I trusted my maker.*

The key word in this relationship is trust. How much do you trust God? Do you *trust* Him to see what is in your heart and to take you into Heaven when you die? If you do, then let me tell you, *you* trust Him.

So how can you trust that it is Him that will guide you in your reformed way of eating? Moses was convinced it was God speaking from the burning bush, but how can you be sure that it's God speaking to you?

The essence of being spoken to, is to listen. The babble of our voices must seem like a child to Him; especially when we praise Him with routine words for one minute or less and then launch into a ten-minute exhortation of Him to help us, with lots of "beseech thee, O Lords," thrown in for good measure!

What we are really asking for in the control of our weight is to be healed. This we can *trust* that He will *do* because it has been *done.*

Who his own self bare our sins in his own body on the tree,
that we, being dead to sins, should live unto righteousness:
by whose stripes ye were healed.*

Notice the second to the last word . . . *were* . . . ye *were* healed. You have only to claim it!

In healing I believe God asks only one thing—obedience. It is by *obedience* that a man who cannot walk, walks. Who cannot talk, talks. It is by obedience that your weight will come off and *stay* off.

To help you with your obedience He will give you two other *gifts,* and there are *no strings attached!* These gifts are knowledge and wisdom.

* I Peter 2:24.

I believe that you can lay claim to these when you pray by saying, "Open my eyes and my heart so that I may see the truth and learn of those things that I must know in order to be obedient."

You may then read His word, the Bible, and look for those scriptures that bear specifically upon your need. Here are a few to get you started, or to remind you of those you already know. This isn't an instant course, it's an appetizer. Try it and see how these work for you *now*, and I say now because you have prayed for Him to open your eyes . . . so that you may see the truth and He will now be *speaking* to you as you read.

Psalms 69:5	Romans 14:14–17
Psalms 141:3–4	I Corinthians 3:16–17
Matthew 17:20	I Corinthians 10:31
Romans 8:5	I Corinthians 10:13
Romans 12:1–2	Philippians 3:18–19

Isn't that wonderful! Thank you, Father, for your Holy Word that is the Sword of the Spirit.

And take the helmet of salvation, and the sword of the Spirit, which is the word of God.*

So now you have two things. By reading His Word, you know what God has in mind for your body, and you have a sword with which to "cut away" those extra pounds, the sword of knowledge in His word.

But we are like Eve when she "saw that the tree *was* good for food and that it *was* pleasant to the eyes," and she went right ahead and disobeyed God's command that she should not eat. We too are tempted every hour of the day by the latest *fruit of the tree which is on the shelves at our local supermarket.* Things that are constructed by man to form a "food that is pleasant to the eye."

We must learn which of these *we* should eat and which *we* shouldn't because *we* are different from each other.

In order to learn we must study. This study is absolutely vital so I would earnestly ask you to write now for the Agricultural Handbook No. 8, U.S. Department of Agriculture, December 1963. It will cost you $2.85 and can be obtained from Bookstore No. 15, P.O. Box 713, Pueblo, Colorado 81002 (att: Mrs. Pichler).

* Ephesians 6:17.

From the same address you can get the up-to-date "USDA Recommended Daily Allowance" which is on the back of "Nutritive Values of Foods"; it will cost you eighty-five cents.

When you receive them I would ask you once again to pray, asking Him: "Open my eyes and my heart so that I may see the truth and learn of those things that I must know in order to be obedient."

Let me give you a brief analogy at this time.

Have you ever seen a person drowning? He splutters, flaps his arms in panic and shouts for help. When a rescuer approaches and tells him quietly, "Roll over on your back and relax. *Trust in me* and I'll get you ashore," what happens? The drowning person starts to *attack* his rescuer. Why? Because he doesn't have *trust,* he just doesn't believe he can be saved!

Now look at you! Are you going to hit out at Him? He has *saved* you and has *healed* you . . . don't fight Him just as He gets to you and asks you to *relax.*

As you open these *lifesavers* and ask that your eyes will be opened you will find a new ability to understand *all* those numbers.

TO "KNOW" IS TO WEIGH WITH YOUR EYES

Each food item is listed as 3½-ounce weights. Three and a half ounces is the equal of one hundred grams in the metric system and grams are the commonly used measurement for all scientific work because they are more easily added and subtracted. (That helps us, not hinders us!)

I believe you should go through Handbook 8 with a fine red felt pen and underline all those foods that you eat from *day to day.* Now go through again with a green pen and underline those you have eaten and feel you *might* want to eat at some time in the future.

It is now *absolutely essential* that you purchase a small weighing scale such as the one-arm balancer that costs only $5 and always measures accurately.

There are other units that sell for $20 and $30. These are more sophisticated and allow you to weigh food up to 14 pounds and to know the metric weight equivalent at a glance.

The point is that you should weigh one hundred grams of each red-underlined food *as you use it* in your daily intake. Take a potato and find out what one hundred grams of potato looks like. You can then look at it and read along the line in Handbook 8 and see *what's in it for you!*

LEARN A LITTLE AT A TIME

Don't try to absorb all the mineral and vitamin contents at one sitting. Concentrate on the calories, protein, carbohydrate and fats, for it is within this quartet that you will need to do the reorganization.

WRITE IT DOWN DAILY

Part of the obedience duty you will have accepted in order to claim your healing will be the constant recording of your progress.

I would suggest you obtain a "Daily Reminder Book" of the type printed by the Wilson Jones Company, selling for $4.40* at bookstores. This you can rule up as follows:

FOOD CONSUMED	QTY.	CALO-RIES	PROTEIN	CARBO.	FATS	(1)
Potato, Boiled (in skin)	3½ oz.	76	2.1 g.	17.1 g.	.1 g.	(2)
Total for the Day		1600	85 g.	150 g.	30 g.	(3)
Target Quantity is		2000	85 g.	150 g.	35 g.	(4)

Weight Today is 195 pounds. (UP) (STEADY) (DOWN) (5)

REMARKS: Very busy day, had no lunch. Sat in front of T.V. after (6)
dinner and fell asleep.

(1) I feel you must fill in the proper headings for at least a month ahead. If you leave pages blank you forget what you are doing and *this you must not do for a single day!*

(2) Use your Handbook for these figures until you know them by heart.

(3) Add up your total accurately—the worst cheaters are the bad adders!

* Price at the time of writing.

(4) Have your own physician fill in this target for you. Tell him you want to lose about eight ounces to one pound per week. A *slow* loss. He will give you the appropriate target quantities.
(5) Weigh yourself *every* day. Never let a day go by! *You expect to lose eight ounces to one pound a week* so your scales won't scream Failure! because you can reduce at this rate with relative ease.
(6) Jot down exactly what you feel your day has been from both a *food in* and *energy out* point of view. This will help you to understand when a dramatic loss or gain takes place.
(7) Buy two books and give one to a friend who shares your weight concern. Suggest that the two of you join together to shed the problem from your lives. Literally mark up your books and compare notes. This helps with the obedience.

DO IT SLOWLY

As I have already mentioned, I believe in gradual weight loss. The loss will be in the region of eight ounces to one pound per week, or an annual loss of twenty-six to fifty-two pounds.

Your physician may advise you to increase this rate of loss and you should follow his advice because only he knows *all* the other differences that go so beautifully to make up your specific needs (in the *natural* sense).

If it is acceptable to lose slowly then do so; in this way your body will firm *up* and not sag *down* as you go.

CAST YOUR NET WIDE, WITH WISDOM

If you introduce *variety* into your meals you will scoop up the needed vitamins and minerals you must have to be in perfect health.

Seek *fresh* variety whenever you can and seek it not from a protein-only vantage point but from the vegetables, fruits, seasonings, dairy or grain products that *go with* the essential proteins. Remember it's the supporting cast that makes the meal, not just the "box office" steak!

FAITH MOVES MOUNTAINS
PROVIDING YOU MOVE IT

For most people "exercise" is as bad a word as "diet." Add the two together and you blow the *self fuse* and fall back on rebellion. The rebel in this case sits down solidly in front of television, says "to Hell with it" (which is splendidly appropriate!) and stuffs himself to sleep!

Exercise routines work for athletes but in our daily lives we seldom associate ourselves with athletics. What we need to do is recognise the need to *move it*. No matter how small the movement, it burns energy and energy comes from our stored fat—providing that the calories we eat are fewer than those we burn.

Once you have established your target (see page 67) with your physician, I believe you should then *move* through your day with physical movement in mind.

Here are some examples:

- Park at least a block away from the store or the office you want to visit and then *walk* over and back.
- At a shopping mall, park on the outer limit and *walk* over and back. You can always *walk* back to the car and drive over to collect your purchases if too bulky to carry.
- *Ride* a bicycle and make short (light burden) trips on it instead of using the car.
- *Climb* the stairs rather than use the elevator if going up or down three to four floors.
- If over four floors, take the elevator to a few floors *below* the one you wish to visit and *walk* up.
- Never leave yourself insufficient time for each "trip." Running short of time leads to *under*exercise.
- If you catch yourself just sitting around, get up and *flap* your arms, *jump* up and down and then sit again; no matter how small the move—you just burned energy and that means *fat*.

In everything you do each day seek active ways of doing it. Be conscious of that old sin of sloth that would lead you to hop a cab for a couple of blocks. The time you *save* could be the time you *lose*—from your life!

RUN YOUR RACE WITH PATIENCE

Immediately discernible weight loss is *not* going to be your reward. You *are* going to lose weight because you do have a great advantage—you have what some folks call "self-discipline" but what I choose to call obedience. We all know that it's the *self* that eventually lets us down but God will never do this to you. Certainly He gives us complete freedom of choice, but when once He is with us, He will never allow us to be tempted beyond our ability to resist.

So, take up the challenge and give it up to God, be obedient and use the knowledge that He has provided in His Bible and His Handbook 8 and His physicians and even in this, one of His cookbooks!

DON'T SUFFER, JUST REFORM

I loathe the word "diet." It suggests a period of deprivation that looks a good deal like suffering. A period that will, eventually, come to an end and we shall be able to enjoy our favorite foods again!

Please understand that with this new approach to right eating, on the first day of your healing you *must* enjoy every morsel of food that you consume. Your "diet" must be a "reform," *a gradual turning away* from the things that have helped to create the excess weight you now carry.

"Reform" is something you will do for all the rest of your life, and stringent self-deprivation is not God's plan. His plan is that you should be relieved of the constant pressures of guilt or failure or both, so that you may be free to love Him. Therefore I feel confident when I say that a quietly determined and gentle change, which we can live with forever, is the answer to our extra pounds.

You have really blessed me by reading these words. I thank you and I stand ready to continue to do all I can to be of service to you within the limits of my natural ability.

May the Lord Jesus Christ be with you in these early days of gentle reform. May the Holy Spirit comfort you and turn your hand from the cookie jar. May God have His way in His great plan for you.

Amen.

SPECIAL NOTE

The words "in many cases" (on page 61) represent a vitally important element in this proposal because it is true that in some cases excess weight may be exactly what God has in mind for you.

Some folk are naturally heavy, if they come from naturally heavy parents and especially if those parents looked upon them as children as "healthy if chubby."

There is very little that can be done for some of these overweight people and to them I would say *seek first your direction from God.* You simply cannot believe any *quick* word that comes uppermost in your mind. You must pray on this quietly, privately and carefully.

In the event that you feel the Lord has "spoken to you" and advised that you are naturally heavy and can only be *unnaturally* slim, then accept this with a joyous heart and simply maintain your weight.

If, after some weeks you fail to find peace and joy in your decision, you may be sure that it was not God who spoke to you.

The Lord's Food Budget

Hand in hand with being a Christian comes the change in attitude that demands the greatest honesty and the most constant prayer; it is in the realm of possessions.

All I can do, or wish to do, is share with you what happened to *me*. This is not a "how to" section—it isn't a blueprint for anyone, it is simply how I feel now and is, I believe, how I shall continue to feel forever:

I am what I am and have what I have and do what I do because God wants it that way.

I am, as a result, no longer *self-employed*. I am employed by Him.

I have, as a result, no talent. My talents are provided by Him.

I own, as a result, *nothing*. His possessions are placed in my care.

My family, as a result, are His. He has placed them under my protection.

Everything I have, all my responsibilities are loaned to me by God.

I am therefore His steward; I shall preserve and guard and cause to multiply His riches and they shall be dispensed as He sees fit.

Because of this, I believe that I have now been released from the "bondage" of my material possessions. If Jesus should pass by and call me, then my family would not only understand but are absolutely willing to set aside all our possessions in order to follow Him.

I am completely and totally sincere about this release and I want to give thanks to Jesus, for He alone made the adjustment.

I share this with you in order that you may somehow see the

problem of the Food Budget from this new perspective. As I said before, it is not a blueprint—it is only a different way for you to look at, or assess; a remedy that works!

Our Food Budget comes out of His total funds and not out of *my* pocket, because I, of myself, am nothing!

He wants us to be properly fed and free from disease.

He does not want us to be overfed, fat and lazy.

He does not want us to waste His riches.

Now that these simple guides are present we find it has an interesting impact upon our purchasing.

- It isn't our money and we don't have to account for it in human terms. We simply have to let our conscience guide us.
- It's no longer a question of saying, "Well, *I* feel like a bit of overindulgence and it's *my* money so why shouldn't *I* do what *I* want with it."
- We look at food for what it will do *within* us. This rapidly dismisses most of the "packaged" foods.
- We are always on the lookout for seasonings that will help less expensive foods to taste better.
- We just love a bargain—*providing it's for a needed commodity.*
- We *never* take money away from the food budget for other "material" purchases. Our budget meets His needs for us; anything less and we are misusing His funds just as readily as we would for an overindulgence.
- We don't use food money for inedibles; neither do we confuse these issues. Most supermarkets will readily ring up two totals for you. All you have to do is separate the edibles from the inedibles.
- We know what we can buy and we buy it to the hilt. When we replace a "packaged food" with a fresh one (see pages 74–75) we apply 50 percent of the saving to the same food budget and the other 50 percent we send to a major famine relief organization so that others less fortunate can share. You may wish to send your donation to an organization supported by your local church.
- We no longer buy vitamin tablets or added chemicals because we seek God's natural provision by buying better, fresher produce.
- We have found a good home for our beautiful big black "Alpo

THE LORD'S FOOD BUDGET · 73

machine," Labrador/mastiff, Jason. Bless his heart—he did *nothing* but ate *everything*. His new owners are hunters and can justify his keep. This is, of course, my decision and need not be yours. "Americans feed their pet cats and dogs enough protein to satisfy the daily requirements of 122 million people, when 14 thousand Indian children go blind each year due to lack of protein!"

- We will not stock up ahead as a provision against an emergency. You may like to look at the Gospel according to St. Luke, Chapter 12, verses 15 to 20 for the reason why.
- We do look at our own garden as a provider by season, from which we can obtain fresh food and also preserve and lay down or give away the surplus. If you haven't got a garden look to glut seasonal prices on *really fresh* produce; lots of savings here.
- When we share our food with others we readily dip into the "Lord's General Fund" because here we share His meat with others in Fellowship. How better would He wish us to use His funds than in Fellowship with His people?
- We do *not* make a "just right" budget do more than it's set up to do—that only results in pulling down the quality of the overall standard.
- We let the budget float *upwards* and *downwards* with the fluctuating rise and fall in the food index. (This of all the items is the hardest to manage and can only be viewed on an annual basis.)
- Finally, we apply as many money-saving hints as possible.

All this concentration results in much better food and it adds to almost every corner of our lives. When we tighten the belt (or at least stop adding new holes!), we gain and gain and gain.

How to Phase Out Cardboard Foods

Firstly a definition is in order. What is a "cardboard food"? Well, I feel it is a food or collection of foods put together in a factory which replaces a food that can be prepared at home by using an easily mastered, quickly executed skill.

Let's go a little further. The food is "cardboard" if it costs more, has less nutritive value, doesn't look, smell or taste as good as the home-prepared food it replaces.

Of course, this doesn't include every food we buy in a can, or a jar, or a carton, or from the freezer, because a good many products do provide us with *time*. Even if the saving is pretty small on a unit basis —the sum total of all of them is substantial.

So what do we do about it?

How's *this* for an idea.

Take out *all* your "cardboard" foods and put them on the kitchen bench. Now, line them up in order of how much time they appear to save *you*.

Example: Instant tea. You need boiling water for both, so it's going to save you the time it takes for the teabag to give up the tea aroma and taste. About sixty seconds in a cup. Four to five minutes in a pot. The time is simply waiting time, there is no *labor* content. This would be a small time saver.

On the other hand, you could get a product that saves considerable non-creative semi-skilled labor time.

Example: Instant potatoes. Here you have a compact product that requires only four to five minutes of cooking as compared with the bulky natural product, which requires washing, peeling, cooking and mashing. You could save some thirty minutes of labor time. This would be a large time saver.

It really does help if you line them up from left to right, starting with the packets that save you the least time and building to those that you *know* save you hours!

But it isn't really that simple. What about those instant products that save a mountain of labor but are fun to make from scratch? How about instant vegetable soup? The time saved can be up to an hour but the pure pleasure *you* might get from assembling the soup could be time well spent.

To help with the decision, since we have all the products out, I suggest that you push those products that you feel have an attractive creative appeal (if made from scratch) back to form a second rank. You can then concentrate upon the front row.

Now, jot down the list of products replacing potentially creative skills in order of their time absorption starting with the minor time savers.

Make a second list of the dull repetitive labor savers, again in order from small to large.

It is important that you make up the list in your kitchen and by your rule of thumb—because it's your time/skill factors we are discussing.

Now—it's adventure time!

Undertake to master one cardboard food skill per week, starting off with the product that will take you the least time to replace and sticking to the order you first wrote down.

Before long you will be making your own yoghurt (page 212), buying bulk spinach (page 191), making your own granola or other superb breakfast cereals (page 198), and using fresh vegetables and fruits. You will finally master the art of making real coffee and real tea. You will combine your own herbs and spices to make your own seasonings and more, much more.

Praise the Lord—*you* will be master of your own kitchen, rich in skills.

A word of warning! Do *not* try to defeat the enemy all at once. Go gradually down the list—stop for a while to let the skills sink in and become perfected; then move on. Also, remember that there are some truly fine instant products that really do help you and give you more time to plow back into your creative kitchen.

SECTION THREE

RECIPES
AND
TECHNIQUES

Recipes and Techniques
to Help You in Your Kitchen

Collected in the next sections are a variety of cooking techniques and recipes that help to enhance aroma, color, appearance, flavor, texture, tenderness, digestibility, good health, weight loss, reduced costs, and hopefully prevent unrewarded effort.

So often we look at the recipe as a whole and forget the careful knowing steps we must take to build a successful final product.

I hope that one or more of the *steps* presented here may find a home in one of your recipes replacing a less satisfactory step you may have taken by habit without knowing why—a step that has robbed you of that satisfaction you get when you know you have done your best for those you love.

These are solid procedures and techniques, not a collection of nifty hints or tricks. All have resulted from my experience over the years, often from failures that I have had personally, and I know of no way that we ever grow but by sharing the blessings of our own shortcomings.

In the past twenty-six years I've made a great many culinary mistakes and have learned from most of them. In this book I offer the solutions and lessons I've arrived at to whet your appetite. Others will follow in our television show, "Take Kerr," and if God is willing, with another collection of techniques.

Key to symbols that appear next to recipes

😊 *THE SENSES* Interesting that when we think of really delicious foods we lift up our eyes. This symbol represents our thanks for the sensual satisfactions of our table blessings.

🌹 *NUTRITION* This symbol stands for the joy of health, freedom from the burden of excess flesh, and vitality through better eating.

💰 *BUDGET* The money bag stands for savings we make through wise food buying—savings we may give in compassion to those who have less than we do.

🕐 *EFFORT EQUALS TIME* When we do things efficiently we save time—time to sit and think and count our blessings. No longer a Martha but a Mary. Luke:38–42

Eggs

💰 *EGGS—do we have a size fixation?*

A quick look at the egg counter in a supermarket will be enough to at least raise a question in your mind. What is the real difference between Extra Large, Large, Medium Grade "A" and Small? We made two identical sponge cakes in the same oven at the same time—the only difference was that one was made with Extra Large eggs and the other with the same number of Medium Grade "A". At the time of purchase the gap between these eggs was 16¢ per dozen (Extra Large 95¢, Medium 79¢ per dozen).* An identical test on soufflés was then run and also worked just fine with no discernible difference. We then bought only Medium for all our work, including "straight eggs." Result? An average 6¢ saving (over mixed large and extra large) per dozen—over 7 dozen per week† = 42¢, or $21.84 per year—to "improve" our reformed food quality.

NUTRITIONAL ADVANTAGE. By using only "Mediums" we do get a small reduction in cholesterol over Large and Extra Large.

SENSE ADVANTAGE does appear to be a little negative, but in actual fact you get used to it very soon. I'm really talking about the "straight egg" (poached, fried, boiled) problem of size fixation. We feel we should have a "big egg" because it looks like all is right with the world. Well, this kind of size fixation, when we don't *need* that extra food, means that all is *not* right with the world!

BUYING NOTES ON GRADES. Egg protein is so near perfection, it becomes a standard to measure other foods.

* Prices at the time of writing.
† 7 dozen included all eggs needed for test and development and normal eating.

"AA" Covers small area; white is thick and stands high, yolk is firm and high. These are good for frying and poaching.

"A" Covers medium area; white is reasonably thick.

"B" Used for general cooking and baking.

BOILED EGGS that don't crack

Various techniques exist to produce a perfectly boiled egg but none so inexpensive and yet so technically perfect as . . . the pin. The idea is simply to equalize the pressure inside the shell when the temperature starts to expand the trapped air. Puncture the blunt end of the eggs (where the air is), put them in a wire basket and lower them all into water that has just been taken off the boil. I believe that eggs should come first and be *followed* by cereals, thus ensuring that the "breakfast cook" can enjoy his or her entire meal with the family.

NUTRITIONAL ADVANTAGE comes, in my opinion, from the fact that the egg has exceptionally high quality protein—so high that it is used as a model for other foods. You get 6 grams of protein per egg and it's a *complete protein*. When you boil the egg you get nothing else added, it's just as God made it and that's how much I trust it and enjoy it daily.

EFFORT ADVANTAGE can be felt by serving everyone with eggs first and then *following up* with cereals and fruit. This way the family shares the table together and that is *vital!*

HARD-BOILED EGGS that shell with no fuss

Whatever way you cook eggs they are better when started at room temperature. Take them out ahead of time or at least warm them for 5 minutes in hot tap water if you forget. One of the finicky jobs in the kitchen is to peel hard boiled eggs. This way it is simple.

Boil water, remove from heat, lower eggs into water in a wire basket or with a slotted spoon and boil gently for 5 minutes. Strain water from the pan and *rustle* the eggs from side to side gently until the shells are cracked all over. Cover with ice cold water (a couple of ice cubes help) for 5 minutes. Then simply twist off the shells. If you cut them open you will notice that there is no darkened green ring around the yolk—we cured that one by cooling the egg quickly.

DILLED EGGS

Halve the egg; lay both sides yolk down on a crisp leaf of lettuce and coat with Light Mayonnaise (page 175) seasoned with dill and cayenne. This can be garnished with two anchovy fillets crisscrossed over the top of each half. Excellent light salad meal that fills the mouth full of flavor.

☺ SCRAMBLED EGGS that can wait

Scrambled eggs are often a problem. The egg solids coagulate and become hard and a watery fluid is left to turn the toast into flab. Really good scrambled are moist, smooth and delicious.

Let's look at a technique that *always* works.

Beat the eggs first in a bowl with a little salt and white pepper. Heat a small quantity (1 teaspoon per serving) of polyunsaturated margarine or butter in a small saucepan over a medium flame. Add the eggs and beat rapidly until they are just set perfectly. Now add 1 tablespoon of *cold* whole milk per egg: assuming 6 eggs for 4 persons, you would use 6 tablespoons (3 fluid ounces) cold milk. Beat the milk in so that it is absorbed by the eggs. The milk will *arrest* the cooking of the eggs and you have only to reheat them *gently* before serving.

APPEARANCE ADVANTAGE is the elimination of *overcooking* and the resultant pool of liquid about hard "curds" of egg protein.

NUTRITIONAL ADVANTAGE is the creation of more bulk with a reduction in cholesterol by total volume. I used to add whipping cream but this was 55 calories and 6 grams of fat per tablespoon. Whole milk is only 10 calories and .5 gram of fat and does exactly the same job at less cost.

SCRAMBLED EGG VARIATIONS

Add some finely chopped small chilis to the pan just before you add the eggs. One level tablespoon per person is fine. They are very hot and obvious, so be sure that everyone likes the idea.

Another idea is to stir in very small cubes of mild cheese when the eggs have set (just before adding the milk); they *just melt* when being served—delicious!

😊 POACHED EGGS *that look the way eggs should look!*

It's such a crying *visual* shame when a poached egg spreads out like a map of North America when it should be oval and full and plump and even. It's also pretty bad when a well-shaped egg tastes like a sponge full of vinegar—or when it's excessively salty. So here is the defense system against such attacks.

Buy the freshest eggs possible for poaching; the fresher they are the more certainly they will hold together. Leave eggs out overnight because the closer they are to room temperature the better. (If the eggs are "old," place them in a wire basket (shell on) and lower into boiling water for 20 seconds. This has the effect of stiffening the egg white or albumen, thereby reproducing one of the conditions of a fresh laid egg.)

Put a little butter into a skillet over a medium flame (1 teaspoon is enough), roll it about to coat the bottom, then add hot water, a *little* salt and 1 tablespoon fresh chopped parsley. Bring to the boil, then reduce to a simmer.

Break and add the eggs in a clockwise fashion—this keeps them in length-of-cooking-time order. Shake the pan gently after adding each egg (called the Amtrack shake because I saw the cook on Amtrack making perfect eggs this way as the train shook the whole galley *gently?*). Allow 3 to 4 minutes per egg until the white is fully set.

Do *not* allow the water to boil; it should just break the surface with rolling bubbles but *not* boil vigorously.

NUTRITIONAL ADVANTAGE lies in the egg's being a "super" source of protein. However, only one egg per head is suggested at breakfasts because of the high cholesterol content.

INTERNATIONAL POACHED-EGG SANDWICH

Toast an English muffin, cover with a slice of cooked Canadian bacon, melt a slice of Swiss cheese on top (under the broiler) and slip a good neat poached egg on top. Dust with parsley and paprika and serve as a hearty breakfast or lunch dish.

(M) *EGG WHITES beaten to a froth that works*

Essential to the success of so many dishes—cakes, soufflés, some special sauces—is the correct whipping of egg white.

I have found a dramatic advantage in using a copper bowl with a loop ring, a wet cloth under the bowl to hold it steady, a little cold water, a pinch of salt and a large flexible hand whisk.

Simply add 1 tablespoon cold water and 1 level teaspoon salt to each 4 egg whites to be whipped and beat in a grease-free bowl *just before they are needed.* You get better volume, it takes less time than the electric machine and the whites *perform* better.

CAUTION: I must caution you about copper bowls. They look nifty but they have one real problem. If the food being placed in a copper bowl is acidic and if the bowl is tarnished, then copper ions will migrate into the food at a level considered unsafe. Accordingly be *Absolutely certain that all your copper is kept tarnish-free!* I wipe out my bowl with salt and lemon skin until it is burnished bright. I then rinse it very well and dry it before use.

NUTRITIONAL ADVANTAGE comes from the fact that egg white provides visual bulk for only 15 calories per egg white. Obviously, the better the eggs are beaten the better they will hold up and work in soufflés, cakes, sauces—in so many different ways. A skillet soufflé is one excellent use because here you avoid the necessity of the *sauce base* called for in other soufflés and thus reduce the fat and calories.

SKILLET SOUFFLÉ

Six eggs serve 4 people. Separate eggs; beat whites. Add 1 ounce (¼ cup) grated cheese per egg yolk to yolks plus salt and pepper. Fold in whites (see next technique) and place in large heated and buttered omelet pan. Fold for 2 minutes with a spatula, then place under preheated broiler to get brown; turn out.

(M) *EGG WHITES folded in correctly do so much more!*

After carefully beating egg whites until they are "peaked" but not dry, many people then proceed to reduce their "spacious" effect by *overmixing* into the basic flavor base.

The best way to avoid overmixing is to add 25 percent of the whites to the base "sauce" and whip it lightly but *well*. This "lightened sauce" is then poured into the egg white bowl and the mix is incorporated by turning the bowl counterclockwise and stirring clockwise with a spoon, lifting the mix up through the center. (See sketch.) Do this very lightly until just combined.

P.S. Don't forget to thoroughly season (over-season) the base "sauce" to compensate for the neutral egg white volume.

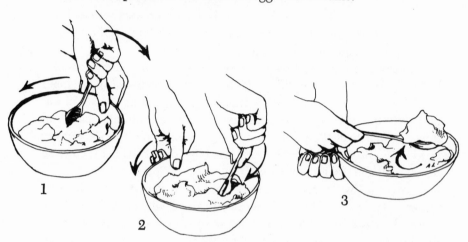

NUTRITIONAL ADVANTAGE comes again from the use of egg whites (at only 15 calories each) to generate visual bulk, thereby cutting back on fats and calories. A large serving of a good Cheese Soufflé provides 471 calories (good); 27.8 g. protein (good); 15.1 g. carbohydrate (good); 15.4 g. saturated fat.

BUDGET ADVANTAGE is very good with soufflés. They can and do provide complete satisfaction at only a fraction of the ordinary cost of fixing an adequate protein dinner.

SWEET SOUFFLÉ OMELET

1. Whip whites of 4 eggs in a basin, adding 1 tablespoon water and ¼ teaspoon salt. Add 2 tablespoons of fruit syrup* and 2 table-

* According to added ingredients.

spoons sugar to the yolks and beat together. When the whites are very stiff, fold in the yolk mixture gently.

2. Add a small piece of butter to a heated pan and wait until the edges of the butter froth. Add egg mixture all at once and stir quickly using a thin metal spatula. Bang the pan on the burner a couple of times to settle the mixture. Smooth the surface with the knife.

3. Place immediately under a moderately hot broiler and lightly cook surface until small bubbles or blisters appear and the level has risen.

4. After the mixture leaves the broiler you can add *your* filling to the center of the omelet. Loosen the edges and carefully fold it out of the pan with the metal spatula. This recipe serves two people. Serve sprinkled with sugar.

Fillings can include fresh peaches, fresh strawberries or plumped raisins and blanched almonds. You can fill lychee nuts with raspberries or use other fresh fruits in a low-fat yoghurt binding. Steer clear of the regular canned syruped fruits and preserves. Their sugar content undoes the benefit.

OMELETS can be detached when they stick

A well seasoned pan (see page 220) is, of course, the best insurance against a "stuck" omelet but if it should catch, then a little butter can be run along the folded side and the mix pried from the pan—allowing the butter to "foam under" and repair the damage. When an omelet is turned out onto a dish, run a little butter over the surface to "glaze" it. This keeps moisture in and improves appearance with very few added calories.

TOMATO AND BACON OMELET
(Serves 4)

12 eggs
1½ cups milk
Freshly ground white pepper
1 clove garlic
Freshly ground salt

Filling:
3 small tomatoes
½ lb. bacon slices
2 tbsp. parsley stalks
½ cup white grape juice
2 tsp. rice vinegar

First prepare:

Mix eggs with milk and pepper. Crush the garlic with salt, and add to eggs. Peel, seed and chop tomatoes to make about 1½ cups. Finely slice bacon. Chop parsley stalks. Measure grape juice and rice vinegar. Now cook!

1. Heat finely sliced bacon slowly in a small saucepan to release natural fats, pour off excess fat.

2. Add tomatoes and white grape juice. Simmer uncovered for 4 minutes.

3. Add parsley stalks and rice vinegar and keep warm.

4. Place a teaspoon of butter in a hot omelet pan. When it foams add the egg-milk mixture and stir rapidly with a fork. Cook until lightly set on the surface.

5. Fill each omelet before folding with a good spoonful of tomato mixture, and turn out as shown in the illustration. Serve very hot.

A special hint: Serve direct from the pan. A tepid omelet is a waste of your energy and your guest's time! (You may wish to say Grace before you begin to cook.)

A FILLED CREPE is better than a stuffed bun!
(or how to make a non-stick pancake!)

By adding 2 tablespoons melted butter to a pancake consisting of 1 cup flour, 1 whole egg plus 1 yolk, and 1¼ cups (9 fluid ounces)* milk, one manages to create (in the right pan, see page 220) a self-buttering pancake that won't stick on turning. The small butter addition also

---

* This mixture is allowed to stand for 4 hours giving finer texture and flavor.

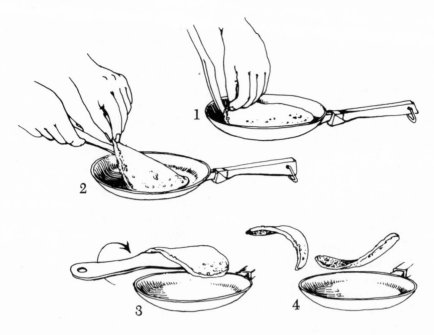

helps to "keep" the finished pancakes when they are made ahead of time and wrapped in a napkin to keep them moist.

NUTRITIONAL ADVANTAGE. The recipe given above produces nine crepes. Each one has the following "profile"; I thought it would be interesting to compare this with a typical hamburger bun because there appears to be a feeling that the crepe is a real diet villain.

	CALO-RIES	PROTEIN	FAT	CARBO-HYDRATE	VITAMIN A
Crepes	104	3.63 g.	5 g.	11.0 g.	277 I.U.
Bun	89	2.5 g.	1.7 g.	15.9 g.	trace

As you see we are only talking about a 15-calorie difference and that's hardly villainous, especially when you consider the variety plus factors.

SENSE ADVANTAGE. A filled crepe (thin pancake) has much more appeal than a hamburger bun (for me at least!)

BUDGET ADVANTAGE comes from a small but satisfactory portion of protein (3½ ounces) of meat, poultry, or seafood) being combined with low-calorie sauces to provide a large attractive portion.

CRÊPES ANTONIN CAREME
("Reformed" from the original)

1 2¾-lb. whole fryer
1 onion, chopped
1 medium carrot, chopped
1 cup sliced celery
4 oz. (1 stick) butter
¾ cup flour
1 cup milk
Salt
Pepper
Nutmeg
1½ cups chicken stock
½ cup white grape juice
2 tsp. rice vinegar
4 tbsp. grated Parmesan cheese
Cayenne
Finely chopped parsley

Crepe Batter:
¾ cup flour
1 whole egg
1 egg yolk
1⅛ cups milk
½ tsp. salt
2 tbsp. butter, melted, for
  batter
1 tbsp. butter, melted, for
  skillet

First prepare:

Make crepe batter—mix flour, egg, egg yolk, milk and salt together until smooth. Allow to stand 4 hours.

Meanwhile cut chicken into quarters; place in large saucepan with onion and carrot. Cover with water, bring to boil and simmer 45 minutes or until tender. Remove chicken from bone; cut meat into small pieces. Reduce chicken stock to 1½ cups. Strain. Cook celery in boiling salted water for 5 minutes; drain and add to chicken.

Now cook!

1. Make crepes by melting 1 tablespoon butter in 8-inch skillet. Place small amount of batter in pan and roll around so that it covers bottom evenly. Cook until waxy bubbles appear on surface, turn with spatula and cook on other side. Remove to plate and continue until 8 crepes are made.

2. Melt butter in saucepan, stir in flour. Whisk in milk gradually to make thick sauce. Season with salt, pepper and nutmeg. Stir in chicken stock and simmer 10 minutes. Stir in new wine (non-alcoholic—see page 217 for method) and simmer 5 minutes longer.

3. Mix 1 cup of sauce with chicken-celery mixture. Stir 3 tablespoons Parmesan cheese into remaining sauce.

4. Place a heaping tablespoon of chicken-celery mixture in center of each crepe. Fold and turn over. Spoon cheese sauce over crepes. Sprinkle with remaining cheese and slide under broiler to brown (about 5 minutes). Dust with cayenne and parsley to serve. Makes 8 servings.

(💰) *DOUBLE BOILERS have prevented disasters for 3,600 years!*

Strangely, the double boiler was first developed in China for a method called *Huann,* in which the juices of ham and chicken are allowed to exit the flesh and form an essence unsullied by any added moisture.

Our kitchen practice uses the double boiler or "porringer" for foods that need to *cook out* over fairly long periods that might otherwise stick or "catch," such as cream of wheat and white sauce; it is also used for *holding* fricassees or sauce-based mixtures ready for serving without scorching. Finally it is used for making egg-based sauces such as Hollandaise and for desserts like the one that follows. Select a clear glass unit in preference to the metal because you can *see the heat** and control it. It costs $10.95 against an alloy example at $12.00.†

---

* By concentration of water bubbles.
† Prices at the time of writing.

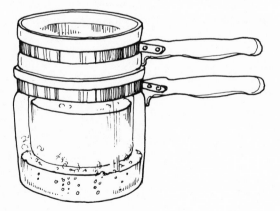

REFORMED ZABAGLIONE

4 medium eggs, separated
¼ cup granulated sugar
¼ cup sweet white grape juice

Method:

1. Cream the egg yolks and sugar with a wooden spoon until very pale and creamlike.

2. Add the grape juice very gently, stirring all the time.

3. Pour the mixture into a double boiler over warm water; the water is heated slowly to a simmer but should never boil. From the moment the mixture is placed over the water it must be stirred with a wooden spoon. Be careful here—scrambled eggs are revolting with grape juice and sugar!

4. The mixture is cooked when it thickens; this should only take about 4 minutes for 4 servings.

5. Remove the double boiler from the heat and allow the mixture to cool.

6. Beat the egg whites stiffly and fold into the cooked yolks. The finished dish should look golden and fluffy.

7. Serve in previously chilled glasses.

Service: If you want to serve this dessert hot, then you have to face up to the fact that into the kitchen you must go. This cannot be cooked in advance, though you can go through step two a good 2 hours beforehand.

Seafood

😊 *SHRIMP COCKTAIL as a splendid first course when entertaining*

In this section I really want to show *two* ways to avoid spoiling this splendid appetizer. Restaurants use a very powerful prepared tomato "dressing" as a sauce dip and they also *couch* the shrimp in a large uncut lettuce leaf as garnish.

I prefer a milder sauce that doesn't overwhelm the delicacy of the shrimp, and I like the lettuce to be in an edible state. Therefore this dressing is mayonnaise-based and seasoned with tomato. The shrimp are bathed in this sauce and laid upon a bed of finely sliced lettuce that has been seasoned with a little salt, white pepper and lemon juice.

APPEARANCE ADVANTAGE. You only need 2 ounces of shrimp per head, and served this way it looks like more, in fact, it looks *great!*

TASTE ADVANTAGE comes from the balance in flavor between the shrimp and the sauce, together with the *cleansing agent* of the lemon-dressed lettuce.

NUTRITIONAL ADVANTAGE is pretty good. The sauce, by using whipped egg white, reduces the normal mayonnaise calories by almost half, and shrimp provides about 26 calories per ounce.

BUDGET ADVANTAGE is reasonable—the cost is about 85¢ per serving.*

* Prices at time of writing.

SHRIMP COCKTAIL

Count on 2 ounces shrimp per person. I prefer the small New-foundland Finger Shrimp to the large frozen ones which, in my opinion, are tasteless. Make up, for 4 servings, ½ cup mayonnaise,* fold into this 1 stiffly beaten egg white, 2 teaspoons of horseradish sauce, 2 teaspoons ketchup, ¼ teaspoon dillweed. This provides 1 cup sauce. Chill well. *Finely* slice some lettuce, mix with salt, pepper and lemon juice and place in a wine glass. Top with shrimp and cover with cooled sauce. Dust with a *little* fresh chopped parsley and paprika. Serve with *thin* slices of buttered wholewheat bread.

MUSSELS are a wonderful variety meal

Mussels are easy and fun and delicious and inexpensive (if you live by the sea!). Maximum price paid should be $1.00 for 1½ dozen but a more reasonable price is about 70¢.†

Here are a few "pointers" that help to make the first experience a happy one:
- Select large shells that are tightly closed.
- Scrub them free from all surface mud, etc.
- Shake each one; if it rattles, discard it—it has a stone inside!
- Grab hold of its "beard" and pull hard; this is much better than leaving them attached only to be dealt with whilst eating.
- When you have boiled them for the 2 minutes and the extra 1 minute (see recipe), look to see if any *haven't* opened. Toss out those that haven't.
- Please respect the advice to strain the "soup" through a cheese-cloth. This removes all the grit and sand that can, so often, ruin a good mussel.

* Mayonnaise can be either homemade or a good polyunsaturated commercial brand.
† Prices at the time of writing.

1 STRAIN JUICE BOIL

2 ADD MUSSELS

3 COVER 2 MINUTES

SHAKE

4 STRAIN JUICE AGAIN

5 MAKE SAUCE

6

SERVE

NUTRITIONAL ADVANTAGE. The food value of mussels is splendid. Here is the profile for 3½ ounces (100 grams) of the mussels, *meat only* —the weight of one dozen good-sized mussels: 95 calories (good); 14 g. protein (good); 2 g. fat (good); excellent iron and iodine.

EFFORT ADVANTAGE. Look closely at the following recipe and you will see that while it may *look* complex it only actually takes about 8 minutes of work to make.

STANDARD "SOUP"

This soup will steam open 80 mussels—enough for 4 portions. You will need:

*2 medium onions (1½ cups
   chopped)*
1 tbsp. garlic oil (see page 160)
1 tsp. thyme
2 tbsp. parsley
2 bay leaves
1 tbsp. whole peppercorns

1 clove garlic
*1½ cups white grape juice and 2
   tbsp. rice vinegar*
¼ cup cream
1 tbsp. chopped parsley
1 tbsp. arrowroot

Method:

Bring to boil all ingredients except cream, parsley and arrowroot, cover and cool. Strain and press out through cheesecloth. (See Illustration, Step 1.) Pour seasoned juice into large pan or split into 2 large pans with tight covers. Bring to a boil and add mussels (see Step 2), then cover and time 2 minutes. *Shake pan well* (hold lid on firmly) and count 1 minute. (See Step 3.) Place cheesecloth in colander and pour soup and mussels into colander. (Step 4.) Dish mussels into a large *heated* bowl.

Pour strained sauce into a pan and bring to a boil. (Step 5.) Combine cream with parsley and arrowroot (*don't add salt*). Stir this cream mixture into the soup, remove from fire, and dish into 4 soup plates. Serve mussels on flat plates with finger bowls. (Step 6.) Use mussel shells as tongs to remove other mussels and drop them into the soup—just fabulous!!

☺ *FISH KETTLE for cooking larger fish whole*

If you should happen to be a fisherman who habitually catches six- to eight-pound fish or if you know someone who does, or if you simply want to cook such a fish for yourself, having bought one, then you'll need a fish kettle.

The most inexpensive kettle is made in tinned steel, is oblong with rounded ends, and has a lid and perforated lifter tray insert. It is so long that it must be placed over two heat elements. Fish are poached in the kettle in a well-seasoned liquid called a "Court Bouillon"—a technique first mastered by the French.

Thoroughly clean the gutted fish by wiping with a damp salt-encrusted piece of cheesecloth. Lay the fish gently in the precooked liquid (see recipe below), cover tightly and turn on the heat to bring to the boil *gradually* (takes about 30 minutes). When it boils, time it accurately at 3 minutes per pound (18 minutes for a 6-pounder). Immediately remove from the stove and allow fish to cool in the liquid for an hour. Remove and serve hot or cold with Light Mayonnaise (see page 175).

NUTRITIVE INFORMATION gathered is interesting; note the relative calories for some of the different fish that can be cooked in this manner. These approximate calorie counts are for a 3½-ounce (100-gram) serving:[*]

Bass	287 calories
Bluefish	192 calories
Catfish	103 calories
Cod	150 calories
Salmon	217 calories
Lake Trout	
under 6½ lbs.	241 calories
over 6½ lbs.	524 calories
Brook Trout	101 calories
Rainbow Trout	195 calories

APPEARANCE, TEXTURE, FLAVOR, AND AROMA ADVANTAGES are extremely high; small pieces of fish when poached just don't measure up (except for fillets of sole).

[*] Charles F. and Helen N. Church, *Bowes and Church's Food Values of Portions Commonly Used,* 11th edition (Philadelphia: Lippincott, 1970). (Hereinafter cited as *Bowes and Church.*)

SIMPLE COURT BOUILLON

*1 large onion (⅔ cup, coarsely
    chopped)*
*2 medium carrots (⅔ cup,
    coarsely chopped)*
1 tsp. oil
7 quarts water

1 cup rice vinegar
⅔ cup coarse salt
2 tbsp. black peppercorns
1 tbsp. chopped parsley
2 bay leaves
½ tsp. thyme

Shallow-fry vegetables in oil, turn into the fish kettle, and add remaining ingredients. Cook over moderate heat for 20 minutes. Strain before using in recipes.

FILLETED FISH with a "fresh-from-the-sea" taste

I learned this simple idea from the Scottish crofters, folk who live in the north of Scotland. They have perfectly fresh fish but use a technique called "crimping" to *revive* fish that might have had a few hours out of the sea and be less than absolutely fresh (like almost all of *ours!*)

Take the fillet and cut shallow light incisions diagonally down its skin side. Place the fillet in ice cold salted water (add 1 tablespoon salt to 2½ cups water). Allow no more than 30 minutes in this salt water; otherwise valuable nutrients can be lost. Lift the fillet directly from the water, dry it and cook immediately whilst it is still chilled.

TOUCH ADVANTAGE is the major plus factor, with many benefits. The fillets are clean, sweet smelling and fresh to the touch—not that old sticky sensation that puts many people "off" fish.

BUDGET ADVANTAGE is felt due to more ready acceptance of excellent *low cost*, complete protein, low fat seafood.

FRIED FISH FILLETS

Lift the fillets directly from the salt water for fried fish fillets. Pat them dry with paper towels and lightly dredge in flour seasoned with salt and white pepper. Shake off surplus and shallow fry in 1:20 sesame/safflower oil (see page 159). Turn once after about 3 minutes, cook on second side and then serve dusted with fresh chopped parsley. Garnish with lemon wedges on the side.

ⓜ *FISH FILLETS can be easily skinned*

Purchasing a whole fish instead of one that is already filleted and packaged can be quite an economy providing that you know how to skin one without leaving your "savings" firmly attached.

Even if you buy the fish filleted there is still one reason why you should consider stripping away the skin. If the fish has been deep frozen for more than 6 months there is a fighting chance that the "oil underlay" beneath the skin has become rancid, which can seriously affect the taste. I suggest you take off the skin *if you are in any doubt.* Simply grasp the tail end of the fillet and place the knife blade carefully between the skin and the flesh (the skin is placed down against the board). Dipping one's fingers into some salt (for a firm grip), hold the blade at about a 25° angle and pull the tail, bringing the flesh over the knife and the skin under in a seesawing side-to-side motion.

NUTRITIONAL ADVANTAGE comes from the fact that we must learn how to make better use of seafood. There are experiments underway at this date in which huge quantities of catfish can be reared in special silos at very low cost. This could well provide food for our futures, but at this time we shouldn't neglect good sources of complete protein at relatively low cost just because we can't *handle* it and are ignorant as a result!

WALLEYED PIKE PIE

Walleyed pike is a classic local specialty of Minnesota. If not available, other solid white-fleshed fish can be used. For 4 servings, strip away the skin and prepare as follows:

1 lb. walleyed pike fillets (or halibut, haddock, flounder, snapper)
1 lb. spinach
6 cooked asparagus spears
2 lbs. potatoes
2 tbsp. butter
1 egg

Freshly ground salt
Freshly ground white pepper
2 tbsp. sesame/safflower oil (page 159)
1¼ cups milk
Parsley and paprika for garnish
½ lemon

Crimp fish and soak in mixture of salt and water for 30 minutes (see page 98).* Wash spinach thoroughly. Trim stems and slice into 1-inch strips. Puree asparagus. Peel and boil potatoes. Mash, adding butter, egg and pureed asparagus; season with pepper and salt. Roughly chop parsley. Oil an ovenproof dish.
Now cook!

1. Place spinach in a large saucepan with 2 tbsp. oil. Season with salt and pepper. Put lid on pan and set over low heat for 5 minutes, giving spinach a good shake after 2 minutes to distribute the oil.

2. Cover the pike fillets with cold milk in another pan, season with white pepper, cover and allow to poach gently for 8 minutes. (Count 8 minutes after you see bubbles around the edge of the pan.)

3. Drain spinach and place half of it in the ovenproof dish. Add

* The colder the salt and water mixture the better. It should almost have ice flakes on top.

drained fish, and sprinkle with juice of ½ lemon. Cover with rest of spinach.

4. Cover spinach with half of the potato, smoothing it with a spatula; then place the rest of the potato in a pastry bag with a star-shaped nozzle and pipe potato decoratively around dish.

5. Bake in a hot oven for 6 minutes until browned.

Sprinkle with parsley and paprika before serving.

A special hint: Be sure to puree the asparagus well. Any "strings" left will clog pastry tube.

($) *WHOLE FISH or can we buy it filleted?*

I knew the answer before I started. Of course, it was beneficial to buy a whole fish and fillet it myself. It *had* to be—how else could they afford the labor, etc., etc.

Of course I was wrong; wrong in New York City that is! In every case, in N.Y.C., supermarket frozen, filleted and packaged fish was clearly less expensive.

FISH		SUPERMKT. FROZEN (FILLETED AND PACKAGED)	FISH STORE FILLETS	FISH STORE WHOLE	BREADED POLLOCK SUPERMKT.
Flounder	Low	1.39	2.00	.95	1.15
	High	1.89	2.80	1.45	2.19
Whiting	Low	.89	2.20	.90	1.15
	High	1.09	2.20	.90	2.19
Lemon Sole	Low	1.35	2.00	1.20	1.15
	High	1.49	3.80	1.45	2.19

These are big-city prices in New York at the time of writing but should indicate the kind of consideration that should be given to fish purchases. In only one case was the whole fish *possibly* a better buy: flounder at 95¢ per pound whole against $1.39 per pound frozen. You should experiment with cutting up a fish to determine the *actual* potential savings of buying whole vs. fillets before you add the labor to your life! When you find the fish that do produce savings keep a note of the edible portion and keep a check on fillet prices.

⏱ BREADING by the two-step method

A well-breadcrumbed piece of fish or chicken is a joy to behold. But the old 3-Step method of flour, egg and breadcrumbs needs some overhaul from both taste and adherence aspects.

We found that 2 whole eggs, 1 tablespoon safflower oil, 1 tablespoon soy sauce and ¼ teaspoon white pepper combined with 2 tablespoons flour makes a fabulous coating before pressing into breadcrumbs for *all* shallow-fried savory dishes without having to mess around with the seasoned flour that tends to create a doughy skin on the fish. The soy sauce on seafood is really excellent. It was, after all, originally designed for such a use in Southeastern China and in Japan.

Poultry

(💲) *CHICKEN versus hamburger—which is the best buy?*

When we look for the best buy I think we have to consider what the word "best" really means. Do we mean literally the *cheapest,* or does it mean the *best-liked* at the *lowest* price. I go along with the latter because I believe that variety and enjoyment generate peace at the table and greater reward for all. We found the following in our tests:

We bought hamburger at $1.00* per pound and a fryer chicken at $2.02* for 3 pounds 11 ounces.

We cooked the chicken *gently* by slow boiling, then stripped off all the flesh (discarding skin and using bones for stock). We got 17 ounces of edible *cooked* meat (11.9¢ per ounce).

To compare this with hamburger, we fried the hamburger and poured off the fat. The cooked meat (less the fat) weighed 13 ounces (7.7¢ per ounce).

We were able to feed 4 people with the hamburger and 6 people with the chicken; there was more apparent size for weight with the chicken. This meant that, for the meat content, the hamburger meal cost 25¢ and the chicken cost 33¢ per head. The chicken was the hands-down winner on appeal and was, in our case, worth the extra 8¢ a serving.

NUTRITIONAL ADVANTAGE lies in a fairly balanced meal in one dish. For 6 servings from the recipe below, "Chicken Lima," we have an analysis per serving of 252 calories (good); 19.6 g. protein; 2.8 g. fat (good); 2.1 g. carbohydrate.

* Prices at time of writing.

CHICKEN LIMA

1 10-oz. pkg. frozen lima beans	*1 tbsp. curry powder*
1½ cups chicken stock	*1 tbsp. arrowroot*
½ cup chopped celery	*2 tbsp. water*
½ cup chopped onion	*16 oz. cooked chicken meat*
2 tbsp. sesame/safflower oil	*1 large apple, sliced*
(page 159)	

Method:

Boil lima beans in chicken stock for 5 minutes; drain, reserving stock. Sauté celery and onion in oil, add curry powder and strained stock. Bring to boil and thicken with arrowroot mixed with water. Stir in cooked chicken meat and heat through. Add apple and lima beans.

💲 *CHICKEN—buy it whole or in pieces?*

When we look at the meat counter for good, inexpensive protein, the lure of the chicken is pretty strong. It comes either in pieces or as a "whole unit." In some cases it can make sense, for a special dish, to buy only legs or thighs but, from the purely economical aspect, you must face up to the fact that you are paying for the extra weighing and packaging. How much is this, in reality?

We discovered that you will pay a premium of at least 6¢ per pound for the "cut up" procedure. There are other, even higher, "bone out" costs, such as chicken breasts with bone left in at 99¢ per pound as compared to fully boned at $1.97.* But all these savings depend upon full utilization of the trim and carcass.

We see this application as saving roughly $10.00 per year if only one chicken is purchased each week.

Here is how a 3-pound raw chicken gets jointed in five minutes, saving at least 18¢ ($2.16 an hour labor, tax-free!).

BUDGET ADVANTAGE springs from the direct savings from doing your own cutting plus the indirect benefit to the quality of your overall cooking by using the carcass and trimmings to make a good chicken stock (see below). The stock can be frozen in ice cube trays for use as required (see page 172).

* Prices at the time of writing.

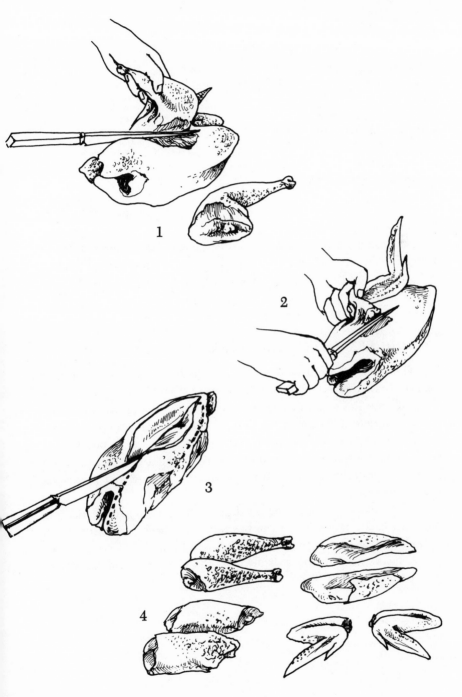

CHICKEN STOCK

*1 tbsp. sesame/safflower oil
    (page 159)
1 tbsp. (½ oz.) fresh ginger root
    (or ½ tsp. dried ginger)
½ lb. chicken feet, bones, neck,
    etc.
½ lb. pork bones (optional—these
    provide a rounder, richer
    flavor)*

*1 3-inch piece of celery
1 bay leaf
Parsley stalk
Freshly ground salt
Freshly ground pepper
8 cups water*

Now cook!

Place oil in a pan, add ginger and fry gently. Add chicken and pork bones, celery, bay leaf, parsley, seasonings and water. Bring to a boil and simmer for 1 hour. Strain. Makes about 4 cups. Cool & skim off the fat before using.

☺ *CHICKEN tied up with only one knot!*

There are all kinds of fancy ways to truss a chicken before it is roasted, braised or boiled, but only one way that uses a single piece of string, no needles and only one knot. But first the reason why.

If you roast a chicken in its natural relaxed manner, without trussing it, there is more area exposed to evaporation, so it dries out. Also, if you rotisserie (spit-roast) the bird it must be held together to retain juices and *baste itself.* It is also neater in every regard and presents a prettier picture.

One important point: You need good string designed for the job. Ask your meat market if you can buy some butcher's twine from them —it's clearly the best! One roll should last a full year.

APPEARANCE ADVANTAGE is obvious—the chicken is compact, even, plump and just looks "juicy."

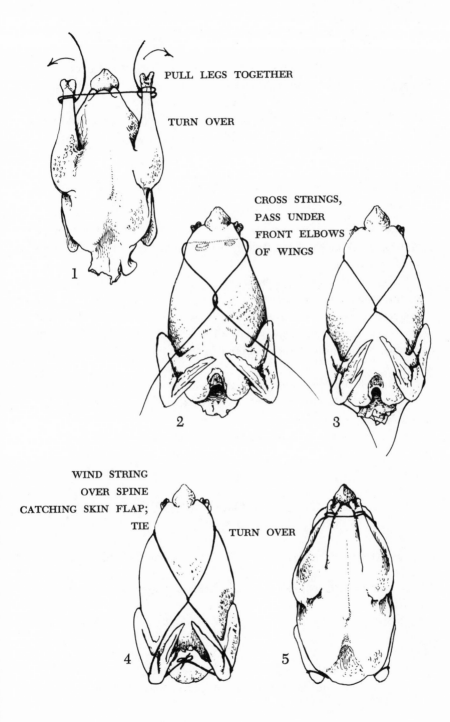

PULL LEGS TOGETHER

TURN OVER

CROSS STRINGS,
PASS UNDER
FRONT ELBOWS
OF WINGS

1

2   3

WIND STRING
OVER SPINE
CATCHING SKIN FLAP;
TIE   TURN OVER

4   5

KAREWAI CHICKEN BARBECUE

Tie chicken in the manner shown above and spit-roast over coals. When almost done, baste well with the following sauce: 6 tablespoons tomato paste, ¼ cup naturally brewed soy sauce, 1 cup chicken stock reduced to ¼ cup by boiling, ¼ teaspoon ground allspice, ground black pepper to taste, 1 teaspoon basil and 1 teaspoon chopped parsley.

Ⓢ *ROAST CHICKEN carved so everyone gets a good shake of the leg!*

The usual idea is to give the legs to the men and the sliced breast to the ladies. Well, since our society is now so preoccupied with equality—let's do better!

Carve off the whole leg with thighs first. Then detach the thigh from the drumstick—4 portions of dark meat.

Carve off the bottom breasts. Cut in at a 45° angle (with the base of the angle behind the wing) across the breast and turn the knife in to cut down and through the wishbone. This gives you two breasts with wings.

Carve off the top breasts. Cut down either side of the breastbone and remove the breast meat intact; serve these with the oyster cuts from under the backbone.

You now have 8 pieces to play with—Equality!

CHICKEN COBHAM STYLE
(*Serves 4*)

1 3½-lb. roasting chicken, plus its giblets	*2 tbsp. naturally brewed soy sauce*
2 tbsp. sesame/safflower oil	*Ground ginger*
6 stalks parsley	*Salt*
	Arrowroot

Method:

1. A good chicken will have its giblets and liver sold with it. Remove the liver and keep it frozen until you have a pâté or a spa-

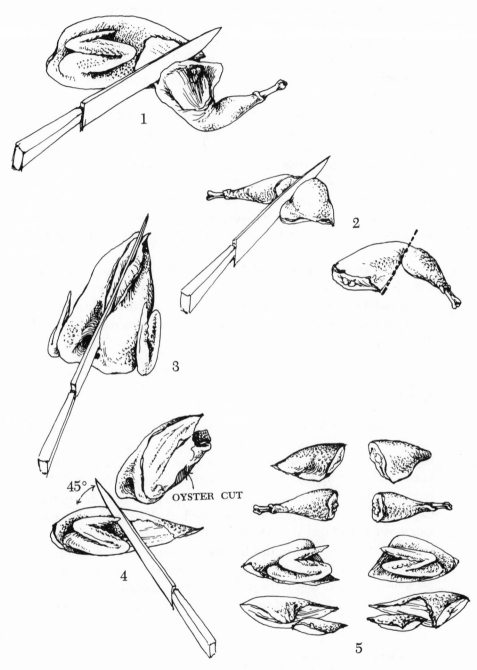

OYSTER CUT

45°

ghetti bolognaise. It can be added to either and gives an excellent flavor boost.

2. Chop up the giblets and brown well in 1 tablespoon of hot oil. Cover with 2 cups of water, add 6 stalks of parsley and allow to simmer until the liquid is reduced to 1 cup. Then add soy sauce to taste, about 2 tablespoons.

3. Truss the chicken (a simple way is shown on page 107), having first seasoned the inside with ground ginger and salt.

4. Mix ½ teaspoon of ginger with 1 tablespoon of oil and brush this mixture over the chicken until the bird is thoroughly coated.

5. Strain the prepared giblet stock into a roasting pan and add the chicken, laid on one side. Cover the bird with buttered paper or foil and roast for 25 minutes on one side, then turn onto the other side for 25 minutes. The oven should remain at a steady 300° F. throughout cookery.

6. Remove the paper or foil and raise the oven temperature to 425 ° F. to just brown the outer skin—for, say, 5 minutes only.

7. Skim the extra fat from the gravy and serve the bird in a shallow casserole with gravy thickened with a little arrowroot (see page 167 for technique).

⑤ CUT UP and cook a 12-pound turkey

The theory behind this technique is the same for all "cut up and cook" segments we have in this book. It is that it can be economical to buy one large unit of meat or poultry for about $7–$8* (gross purchase price) and cut it up from the fresh state into specific "mini cuts" that can be cooked by a variety of different techniques. That this system can save you money is practically self-evident. That it can also provide greater flexibility than the leftovers from, say, a whole roasted turkey is also clear. Add to this the added nutrients, flavor, moistness and texture and, apart from the skill and effort element, you've really got it made. So here now is the skill factor that makes it possible to get 16 portions over 4 different meals at an average cost per serving of 43.4¢.†

---

* Prices at the time of writing.
† A 12-pound 9-ounce turkey at 59¢ per pound costs $7.41.

CUTTING INSTRUCTIONS FOR TURKEY

1. Position turkey on its back, as shown. Cut along dotted line to detach drumstick and thigh. Pull away and down, making cut between the seam that joins the thigh and drumstick to the carcass.

2. After the initial cut, pull the drumstick and thigh down and away from the carcass while holding with other hand. This will expose the joint where the thigh is joined to the carcass. Insert knife blade at the center of joint and cut down along dotted line (as illustrated) until leg and thigh are detached. Repeat procedure for the other leg and thigh.

3. Now remove the turkey breasts by cutting along the dotted lines shown. Cut closely to the breast bone on both sides all the way down to the bottom of the rib cage where the wing joins the base of the breast.

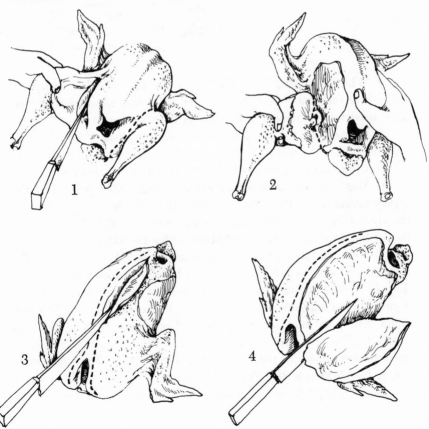

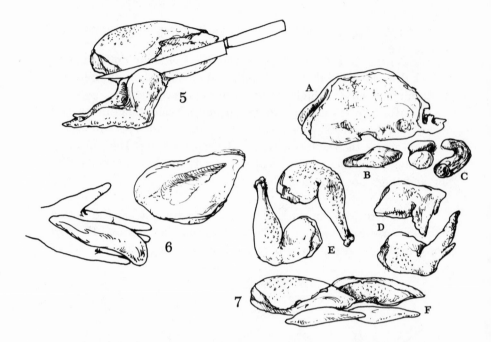

4. Where the wing joins the breast, we have another joint. Cut through at the center point of the joint until the breast portion and wing are detached. Repeat procedure for the other breast.

5. Now detach the wings from the breast portions. This is done by first extending the wing, as shown. Cut through at angle shown to detach wing, cutting away as little of the breast meat as possible.

6. Here the left hand is holding the tender fillet portion of the turkey breast called the "supreme," and the right hand is pointing to the area of the breast from where it was removed. It lies in the *inner* part of the breast and is easily lifted out without cutting.

7. Here we have all the portions assembled. First, we have the carcass A which can produce four pints of jellied turkey stock. This is done by gently simmering the carcass in eight pints of water for four hours. Do not add any seasoning until you actually use it. You can strain and pour into ice cube trays, freeze and then place in a plastic bag for later use. It will also make a delicious soup for four by thickening with rice or potatoes or mixed vegetables. B is 4 ounces of turkey liver which is just like chicken liver. It has an excellent flavor and can be chopped up and stirred into rice for chicken liver risotto.

The next pieces C are giblets and the neck which can be added to the carcass for some good stock. We then come to the two wings D for BBQ Turkey Wings. Next are the two breasts E for Braised Turkey Breast, which are cooked by moist heat to retain the breasts' moisture and tenderness. The two supremes F are poached gently in Supreme of Turkey Cornell. And, last, the drumstick and thigh G are great in Turkey Lima, which serves at least four people.

FREEZING—See page 121 for correct freezing technique.

BBQ TURKEY WINGS
(Serves 2)

2 turkey wings (detached from the breast at the wishbone)
¼ cup tomato ketchup
1 tbsp. rice vinegar
1 tbsp. naturally brewed soy sauce

3 cups turkey stock (made from carcass)
1 large clove garlic
1 tbsp. chopped parsley stalks
1 tbsp. safflower oil

First prepare:
Cut wings into three pieces each at the natural joints. Measure ketchup, soy sauce and turkey stock. Peel and crush clove of garlic. Chop parsley stalks.
Now cook!
1. Combine turkey stock and turkey pieces.
2. *Simmer* the wings for 40 minutes in the turkey stock in a covered pan until *just* tender. Remove meat and pat dry with paper towels. Reserve ¼ cup stock.
3. Heat safflower oil in small skillet; add cooked turkey pieces and brown.
4. Add garlic and ketchup. Cook, stirring, until the ketchup is deep brown, then add ¼ cup stock, soy sauce and vinegar. Cool in the sauce.
5. Using tongs, place coated turkey pieces under (or over) broiler to heat through and become glazed. Dust with finely chopped parsley stalks and serve with finger bowls to help clean up your hands—there's no other way to eat them!

SUPREME OF TURKEY CORNELL
(Serves 2)

3 cups turkey or chicken stock
¼ cup whipping cream
¼ cup small white mushrooms
1 tbsp. arrowroot
1 tbsp. naturally brewed
 soy sauce

1 tsp. fresh lemon juice
1 tbsp. chopped fresh
 parsley leaves
2 6-oz. turkey supremes (inner
 fillets of breast)
1 tsp. paprika

First prepare:

Measure stock, cream. Weigh, wash and dry mushrooms and cut into quarters; measure arrowroot and combine with soy sauce; squeeze lemon; chop parsley, finely.

Now cook!

1. Lay the supremes in a shallow skillet; add the stock and cover tightly. Poach over a low heat for 8 minutes until just cooked without undue shrinkage.

2. Remove the supremes and keep them warm. Boil the poaching liquid vigorously to concentrate its flavor until only 1 cup is left.

3. Add the mushrooms to the reduced stock and boil 60 seconds only. Add the lemon juice and pour in the soy-arrowroot mixture; let it thicken, just coming to a boil. Remove from heat. Now add the cream very slowly, stirring all the time. Add parsley and return the supremes to the sauce—heat through but do not boil and serve, dusted with paprika, on a shallow dish.

BRAISED TURKEY BREAST
(Serves 4)
(Note that, as the turkey has
2 breasts, it will eventually
serve 8.)

2 oz. bacon slices
1 large carrot (5 oz.)
1 large onion
¼ cup tomato paste
1 cup turkey or chicken stock
1 tbsp. rice vinegar
½ cup white grape juice

2 tsp. arrowroot
1 tbsp. chopped parsley
1 turkey breast (2 lbs.)
 (minus the inner fillets)
1 tbsp. naturally brewed soy
 sauce
1 bay leaf

First prepare:

Cut bacon in 1-inch squares. Peel and slice carrot and onion. Measure tomato paste, turkey stock, grape juice and rice vinegar. Measure arrowroot and combine with the soy sauce. Chop parsley. Preheat oven to 300° F.

Now cook!

1. Heat bacon in dutch oven to release fat. Remove the bacon pieces and color the turkey breast in the bacon fat (5 minutes at medium-high heat on each side). Cover the pan for best results.

2. Remove the meat, replace the bacon and add the carrot and onion. Fry 2 minutes. Add tomato paste, stir well and cook until the tomato browns.

3. Add turkey stock, grape juice and bay leaf. Return meat to the pan, cover and place in oven for 50 minutes. Test for tenderness—it should be just underdone. Strain the "sauce" through a sieve, pressing out the moisture but *not* pushing through the softened vegetable fiber.

4. Skim off *all* fat. Bring sauce to the boil and thicken by beating in the arrowroot-soy sauce mixture. Adjust the seasoning. Add rice vinegar. Carve the breast into 12 thin slices (it should be slightly pink), reassemble into the breast shape in a shallow serving dish (with lid) and coat with the finished sauce. Garnish with boiled small onions and carrots and sprinkle with parsley.

TURKEY LIMA
(Serves 4)

2 turkey legs and thighs (2 lbs. meat)	1 tbsp. arrowroot
	2 tbsp. water
1½ cups turkey stock (made from carcass)	1 8-oz. package frozen lima beans
1 stalk celery	2 tbsp. safflower oil
1 small onion	1 tbsp. curry powder
1 large apple	2 tbsp. chopped fresh parsley

First prepare:

Detach drumsticks from thighs and cook both in turkey stock (for preference) or water *if you must* until tender—about 1 hour. Remove the skin, strip flesh from bone and cut into even-sized strips; keep moistened with cooking liquid. Finely slice the celery and onion and apple. Measure and mix the arrowroot and water.

Now cook!

1. Boil the lima beans lightly in turkey stock for 5 minutes, then drain.

2. Shallow-fry the celery and onion in the safflower oil with the curry powder; add the strained stock. Bring to the boil and thicken with the arrowroot mixture. *Vegetables must remain crisp.*

3. Stir in the turkey and allow to heat through. Add the thinly sliced apple and the bright green lima beans. Turn into a shallow earthenware dish and serve immediately, dusted with parsley.

Meat

☺ *BUTCHER'S KNOT can help you in so many ways*

This is one of the truly basic skills that can mean so much in your kitchen. It helps you to do your own cutting up, which saves you a good deal of money. It lets you untie what the butcher did and season or stuff the rolled piece to make it taste better or go further. This is how it's done:

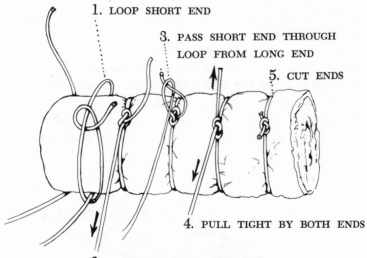

1. LOOP SHORT END

3. PASS SHORT END THROUGH LOOP FROM LONG END

5. CUT ENDS

4. PULL TIGHT BY BOTH ENDS

2. PULL TIGHT BY LONG END

SENSE ADVANTAGE comes largely in the fields of appearance and flavor. A well-boned and -tied roast just looks terrific and it's much easier to carve without ugly and difficult-to-negotiate bones. The flavor is improved by seasoning from the inside out—a technique that simply must be better than "surface crop dusting"!

BEEF SEASONING FROM THE INSIDE

Mix ¼ teaspoon each of cinnamon, cardamon, nutmeg and black pepper with 1 teaspoon of ground ginger and 3 crushed cloves of garlic. Spread this "paste" evenly upon the cut surface of a 3- to 4-pound rolled beef roast, then roll tightly and retie as shown. You can modify the seasoning for lamb or veal breast—all manner of super flavorings are yours to invent and use.

CARVING *can be more rewarding in the kitchen*

Traditionally the "man of the house" carves in the dining room for his family. Is this really such a good idea? Firstly, a roast large enough to serve 6 to 10 people at Thanksgiving looks great. But a 2-pound roast for 4 people doesn't look appealing—it looks like the man of the house isn't providing!

Secondly, with all the "fiddling about," the food tends to get cold. I believe in carving in the kitchen, laying the meat on an oval dish, reheating it in an oven or over boiling water covered with foil, coating it with natural juices (not fat) and garnishing it with some of the vegetables—all *steaming* hot. This way we get speedy hot service, even distribution of servings, *excess fat cut away*—and it looks super.

BUDGET ADVANTAGE. This idea helps the budget by reducing unnecessary cooking of a larger cut (see below).

NUTRITIONAL ADVANTAGE. I like to thicken my meat juices and add to them some of our stock cubes (see page 172). We must drain *all* the fat from the roast pan, add the stock cubes and bring to the boil—scraping up all the meat residues. We then add arrowroot (see page 167 for the technique) and a little parsley and pour into a sauceboat. We *brush* the meat with this gravy sauce rather than smother it. In this way a "reformer" in the family can get a fair chance at sticking to his or her guns!

💰 ROAST only what you need!

The use of cold roasted meats in leftover dishes is, in my opinion, the most wasteful practice in the North American kitchen. A family of 4, for example, will purchase a 4-pound roast of beef for a family dinner. It will cost about $2.50 per pound or a total of $10.00. After roasting it will weigh about 3 pounds—at $3.33 per pound. Each person likes to see about 5 ounces (cooked weight) of sliced beef; for our family of 4, we like 20 ounces. This leaves 28 ounces *surplus to requirement* at $3.33 per pound—or $5.60 for 1 pound 12 ounces of cold roasted meat! Either it is eaten up at the meal *in excess of even our emotional needs* or it is used as "leftovers" within another recipe that could easily have used say hamburger at $1.00 per pound with a subsequent saving of $2.33 per pound!!!*

NUTRITIONAL ADVANTAGE. Dietary surveys indicate that Americans are not lacking for protein in the diet. In fact, *even in underdeveloped countries* the problem of malnutrition seems to be associated with total calories available and not only with protein. We are "hung up" on protein, and specifically on meat. Protein is an important nutrient but most of us greatly exceed our *needs*. Protein eaten in excess of bodily needs is either used for energy—that is, burned as calories—or stored as *fat!!!* if the energy is not expended. In this context, excessively high meat consumption, as with any food, is *fattening*.

BUDGET ADVANTAGE. Depending upon how often you roast meat, you could save considerable amounts of money. I once was able, by instituting this theory in a large-scale catering responsibility, to save about $153,600 in an overall budget of $5,700,000—or nearly 3 percent

---

* All prices at the time of writing.

of the total. You might manage the same with your total budget.

SENSE ADVANTAGE. There is a fall-off in visual appreciation through the miserable-looking little roast, not at all the sort of thing we associate with the front cover of the *Saturday Evening Post!* But, take heart —see page 117 for a way of avoiding this problem.

To ROAST WHAT YOU NEED, order your roast next time by multiplying the number you will feed by 8 ounces—i.e., for 4 people, 4 × 8 ounces = 2 pounds of *boneless* meat. Roast it at 325° F. and carve in thin slices. If this works *then* reduce the quantity until you sense an adverse reaction—and may God bless your efforts!

⑤ *COOKING AHEAD and using the freezer*

The bulk precooking of a single, delicious casserole so that in one afternoon one makes the base for eight fully flexible dinners for four people isn't a bad project—especially if the family can be pressed into service!

The concept needs a good deal of explanation so let's get into it.

THE POT. Absolutely essential to this idea is a large cooking pot. We thought this out carefully and looked at all the large pans on the market. We settled on the inexpensive enameled clam cookers that hold truly vast quantities. We suggest one that will fit into your oven and will hold at least 10 quarts (2½ gallons). It can be used for other work when boiling large chickens, or cooking a ham, steaming clams, boiling a lobster, even as a water bath for preserving.

THE MEAT. Select a cut that has good connective tissue content (i.e., it works hard—like the neck and shoulder muscles of lamb, pork, and veal). It should be a "young meat" like veal or pork or lamb because it can be "finished" in a greater variety of ways than beef or mutton. I selected as a test unsmoked picnic hams weighing about 20 pounds and costing only 75¢* per pound. *True*, they have to be boned and skinned, but this way you control the fat content and the size of the pieces (12 2-inch cubes—3 each for 4 persons), and you get the bones for the broth. After discounting the trim and bones the cost doubles, to $1.30 per pound, *but* you get good lard—at least 1 pound— and this costs about 27¢ per pound. You also have 5 pounds of bones that can replace about 50¢ of flavor material gained otherwise from stock cubes or powders.

---

* Price at the time of writing.

THE JUICE. This is the vital difference in *our* technique. We believe that vegetables cooked and then frozen and then reheated are *awful*. Thus we make our stock with the bones (from which you've trimmed the meat), 2 pounds onions, 2 pounds carrots and 1 pound celery, all roughly chopped, ¼ cup safflower oil, 8 bay leaves, 1 tbsp. thyme, 8 cloves garlic, 2 tbsp. salt, 2 tbsp. ground black pepper, 6 quarts water. Roast the bones in the big pan in the oven at 375° F. until nicely browned. Drain off the fat. Fry the vegetables in the oil in the big pan until limp, then add the rest of the ingredients. Cover and place in 350° F. oven for 1 hour. Strain. Throw out vegetables and herbs (they are totally without value at this stage) and retain bones in broth which should now measure about 10 pints. You can make this stock while you are cutting and trimming the meat.

THE MEAT. The meat must be fried in a little garlic oil in a hot skillet, piece by piece, until well colored. Then turn directly into the big pot containing the hot strained stock plus bones. When filled, cover the pot and cook 1 hour at 350° F. The meat will then be completely cooked, an essential for pork. The fat must be carefully skimmed off, which will leave approximately 8 pints.

WRAPPING AND FREEZING. The meat must be laid on a shallow tray to lose heat *quickly*. Select a dish approximately 8 by 5 by 2 inches. Line it with foil 3 times its length (i.e., 24 inches long). Press foil into the "mold," fill each dish with ⅛ of the cooled mixture (12 pieces of meat, plus juice), fold the ends over and roll the edges together (see illustration). *Label and date* 3 months hence; this is the date by which it must be eaten. Lift onto baking sheet and slide into deep freeze. Have free space around each one to hasten freezing (you can stack them later). Foil costs 75¢ for 75 feet, thus each packet costs 2¢ to wrap.* Meat must be kept at 0° to −10° F. to be safe, and then for no more than 6 months. It's very important to freeze promptly and to use sanitary handling practices—e.g., don't handle cooked meat with utensils used to handle raw meat.

RESUSCITATION. Divide your recipe ideas into 3 groups.
- *Spice Fry Off:* Curries, chili. Fry onions first with spices for 10 minutes. Add frozen meat, cover pan and cook slowly to defrost and heat through, say 10 minutes. Thicken with arrowroot and serve.
- *Root Vegetable Precook:* Cook fresh root vegetables such as po-

* Price at the time of writing.

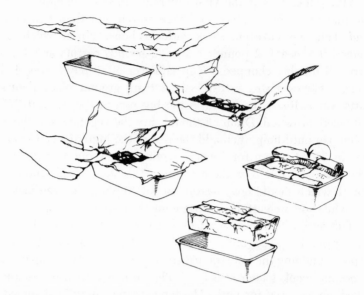

tatoes, turnips, carrots, etc. in a little oil with tomato paste for color; add a little water. Cook 10 minutes, then add frozen meat. Cook over low heat to defrost and heat through—about 10 minutes. Thicken and serve.

Pre-made Sauce: Defrost over low heat for 10 minutes. Drain, reserving all liquid. Add small vegetables (peas, etc.). Cook the vegetables in the broth. Thicken with cream or milk and arrowroot, then add the meat and heat through.

⑤ *HEAT PRONGS may help*

Since the increasing cost of living for both fuel and food has hit us we are being besieged by the "Heat Prong" as an economy-oriented proposal.

Heat Prongs work by carrying heat *into* a large muscle or dense object, like a potato, and by conduction hastening the cooking from the inside out as well as the normal outside in. The question is, does this save time and money?

Potato Nails resulted in 5 minutes less baking time, when used from both ends. The Hang and Bake strips (in which the prong is twisted to hold the potato as it hangs from the oven rungs) didn't work. The test on the Cooking Pin* was, however, interesting. We took 2 similar rolled loins of pork, one with a Pin in, one with no Pin. Side by side roasting at 325° F. for 90 minutes resulted in our usual satisfying perfectly cooked roast without the Pin. But with the Pin, the roast was overcooked badly. Later tests revealed a 15-minute saving of time from use of the Cooking Pin with a resultant weight saving of 1 ounce. All you have to do is ensure that the tip of the Pin is higher than the black knob and that no part of the pin touches anything other than the meat or clear air (avoiding the bone, for example).

BUDGET ADVANTAGE. One ounce on 1 pound 12 ounces equals a 1/28 saving; at $2 per pound the savings equals 7¢ (at 1 roast for 4 per week)—and 7¢ per week equals $3.64 per year. Unfortunately that's less than the pin costs!† I used this whole examination to prove a point. We may well be attracted to what appears to be a logical little gadget but it is my experience that, armed with a meat thermometer (see below) and a portable timer (page 220) and an oven with an accurate thermostat—all you need as gadgets are two hands and a brain!

SENSE ADVANTAGE. One disadvantage here is that the pin cooks the meat well done or close to it. In this way it isn't possible to get meat cooked rare, unless you can put up with a roast with rare rings!

(💰) *MEAT THERMOMETERS tell you more than temperature*

Described by all modern authorities as an *essential*. This simple instrument can save a great deal of money when used in association with an in-oven thermometer and a set of scales. You need to know exactly how much the meat weighs and that your oven is accurate at 325° F. which is the temperature most suited to most dishes.

A good thermometer will cost about $3 to $6, with the professional one about $19. Consider two things about the unit. First, you should select a unit with a large head; that is, the dial needs to be about 2 inches in diameter. These cost about $6. The head must be large so that there is enough air to expand without destroying the dial when left in the oven for the full cooking time. (The professional model at about $19 reads almost instantly, but this is *not* for home use. The professional uses it to jab in *large* cuts to confirm his opinion. To keep

---

* This is a heat-conductive fluid-filled prong about 9 inches long that is used to prod into meats.
† Prices at the time of writing.

on jabbing at a domestic cut will drain out the juices, and if you leave the professional one *in,* its small dial will be destroyed due to there being insufficient room for the air in it to expand.) Second, you must place a thermometer in the meat correctly, with the dial facing you from the oven. The point must be in the middle of the muscle and not touching a bone. The dial must not be closer than 3 inches to an overhead oven element. Lastly, they don't work in microwave ovens.

NUTRITIONAL ADVANTAGE. Studies done on rare and well-done roast beef indicated a higher retention of B vitamins when cooked to the rare stage. Thiamin is particularly sensitive to heat and is reduced the most when beef is cooked to the well-done stage.[*]

(💰) *CUT UP and cook a 6½-pound boneless beef chuck roast*

This is the second in our series on getting more out of a large cut by being your own butcher (see pages 111–13 and 138–39 for other techniques). Here we get some great value by cutting 18 portions for 4 different meals for an average cost of 41¢ per serving.[†]

[*] Ruth M. Griswold, *Experimental Study of Foods* (Boston: Houghton Mifflin, 1962).
[†] Beef chuck cost $1.19 per pound and weighed 6 pounds 3.2 ounces for a total of $7.38—price at time of writing.

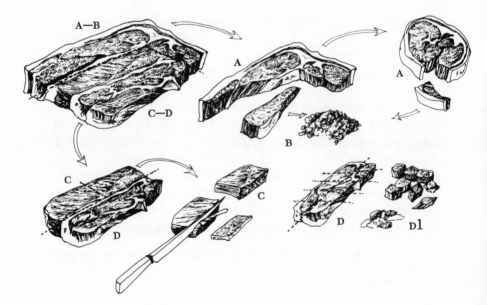

CUTTING TECHNIQUES
FOR BEEF CHUCK ROAST

1. Place roast on cutting board. The dotted lines show how the roast is to be cut.

2. Cut along dotted line to separate A-B from C-D. A-B is now an L-shaped piece. Cut B away from A and grind B and the little "tail" from A for the Stuffed Sourdough Meatloaf.

3. Portion A, rolled, is for the Pot Roast.

4. Cut C-D along dotted line to separate C from D.

5. C is the steak portion. Put it in the freezer section of the refrigerator to chill for at least 45 minutes. This will make the meat easier to slice.

6. After C has been chilled, it should be cut in half with the grain. Then cut each half in thin slices across the grain as shown. You should get six slices from each half, a total of twelve, for the Playing Card Steaks.

7. D is to be cut along dotted lines into eight 3-ounce pieces of stew meat for the Napa Valley Casserole; Any extras, D1, are diced fine or minced for the Stuffed Sourdough Meat Loaf.

8. Wrap portions tightly in freezer wrap and refrigerate or freeze for future use. Mark the portions with names of recipes.

FREEZING. See page 120 for correct freezing technique.

Four simple recipes for the main cuts obtained are as follows:

POT ROAST
(Serves 4)

1 2½-lb. pot roast cut
2 oz. bacon slices
1 large carrot
1 large onion
1 large clove garlic
¼ cup tomato paste
½ cup beef stock

½ cup red grape juice (see page 218)
1 tsp. cold, unsweetened tea
1 bay leaf
2 tsp. rice vinegar
2 tsp. arrowroot
2 tbsp. water
1 tbsp. chopped parsley

First prepare:

Cut bacon in 1-inch squares. Peel and slice carrot and onion. Crush garlic. Measure tomato paste, beef stock, grape juice, tea, and vinegar. Measure arrowroot and combine with the water. Chop parsley.

Now cook!

1. Heat bacon in dutch oven to release fat. Remove bacon pieces and color the pot roast cut in the bacon fat (5 minutes at high heat on each side). Cover the pan for best results.

2. Remove the meat, replace the bacon and add the carrot and onion. Fry 2 minutes, add garlic and fry 1 minute more. Add tomato paste, stir well and cook until the tomato paste browns.

3. Add beef stock, grape juice, tea, vinegar and bay leaf. Return meat to the pan, cover, bring to a boil and place into an oven set at 325° F. to cook for one hour. Test for tenderness—remove the meat if cooked. Strain the sauce through a sieve, pressing out the moisture but *not* pushing through the softened vegetable fiber.

4. Skim off *all* fat. Bring sauce to the boil and thicken by beating in the arrowroot mixture. Adjust the seasoning. Replace the pot roast cut to simmer for 15 minutes in the sauce before serving.

5. Garnish with long sliced boiled carrots seasoned with nutmeg, and small dumplings. Dust the pot roast with parsley just before presentation.

PLAYING CARD STEAKS
(Serves 4)

1 1-lb. center cut of chuck (cut into 12 slices)	4 tbsp. soy sauce
	1 lb. green noodles
2 cloves garlic	1 tbsp. safflower oil
1 tsp. ground ginger	

First prepare:

Chill the meat in the deep freeze until it is quite firm (about 1 hour). Being sure to cut *across* the grain—not with it!—cut the piece in two equal cubes (each about 3″ x 2″) and slice each cube into 6 "playing card" slices, as shown in illustration on page 118. Crush the garlic and combine it with the ginger and soy sauce. Brush this marinade/baste onto the steaks.

Now cook!

1. Cook the noodles as indicated on the package.

2. While they are boiling, heat a large skillet and add the oil. Lay the marinated slices in the pan and fry briskly on both sides to color.

3. Dish the green noodles and set the steaks around the mound (the steaks only take 60 seconds to cook).

STUFFED SOURDOUGH MEAT LOAF
(Serves 6)

1 loaf sourdough or French
* bread, about 4" x 14"*
2 tbsp. butter
2 cloves garlic

Filling:
1 medium onion
1 clove garlic
¼ cup tomato paste
¼ cup soy sauce
¾ cup water
1 tbsp. safflower oil
1 lb. finely chopped or home-
* ground beef*
1 tbsp. chili powder
1 tsp. oregano

First prepare:

Peel and chop onion. Crush garlic (keeping cloves for bread and for filling separate). Measure tomato paste, soy sauce and water. Now Cook!

1. Sauté 1 clove garlic and onion in oil.

2. Add beef and cook until meat changes color; drain excess fat from pan.

3. Add tomato paste; cook until it begins to brown. Add chili powder, soy sauce and water.

4. Cover, reduce heat to low and simmer 30 minutes. Add oregano.

5. While meat is simmering, remove center from bread loaf by hinging back the top and spooning out the bread. Leave about ½-inch wall all around.

6. Melt butter, add 2 cloves garlic and brush on inside of loaf.

7. Spoon in chili mixture and cover with Hot Bean Dressing (recipe follows).

8. Replace top of loaf. Heat at 350° F. for 20 minutes, until loaf is brown and crusty.

9. Cut diagonally to serve.

HOT BEAN DRESSING

1 cup dried red kidney beans	1 tbsp. chili powder
1 smoked ham hock (12-oz.) bone in	½ cup sour cream
	1 fresh red "hot" chili pepper
4 slices bacon	2 tbsp. chopped bread-and-
1 medium onion	butter pickles

First prepare:

Soak the beans in cold water for 24 hours. Then place in clean fresh water with the ham hock and bring *very slowly* to the boil (should take about 30 minutes). Now reduce heat to simmer and cook for another 1½ hours until beans are tender. Allow to cool in the stock, ready for use. Chop the bacon finely; peel and finely dice the onion. Measure the chili powder and the sour cream.

Now cook!

1. Fry the chopped bacon with chopped onion—no need to add any oil.

2. Add the chili powder and continue to fry for one minute. Add the drained cooked red beans; stir gently. Pour on the sour cream and cook gently over a low heat for 30 minutes more, until the beans have partially absorbed the "sauce." Serve hot or cold with the chopped pickles and chili peppers stirred in at the end. Or the pickles and peppers can be served in separate small dishes to be added according to preference by the individual at the table.

Note: This is a general recipe that can be used to spice up other dishes, especially Mexican or Spanish ones.

NAPA VALLEY CASSEROLE
(*Serves 4*)

1 1½-lb. lean chuck steak
2 large carrots
2 medium onions
1 small parsnip
¼ cup tomato paste
2½ cups beef stock
1 bay leaf
1 tsp. dried thyme (or 3 or 4
*   sprigs fresh)*
6 parsley stalks
1 4-inch celery stalk
½ cup red grape juice (see page
*   218)*

1 tsp. cold tea
1 tbsp. arrowroot
1 tbsp. soy sauce
¼ cup sesame/safflower oil (page
*   159)*
Salt and pepper
2 tbsp. chopped parsley
2 tsp. rice vinegar

Garnish:
8 small carrots
8 small onions

First prepare:

Cut lean chuck steak into 8 3-ounce pieces. Peel carrots and cut into large pieces. Peel onion and cut in quarters. Peel parsnip and cut into large pieces. Measure tomato paste and beef stock. Tie bay leaf, thyme, parsley stalks and celery stalk (or use muslin or cheesecloth bag if dried loose herbs are used). Measure red grape juice, tea and vinegar. Measure arrowroot and combine with soy sauce. Peel small onions and carrots and leave whole.

Now cook!

1. Prepare this dish in a heavy ovenproof casserole or ovenproof saucepan which can also be used with high heat on top of the stove. Preheat oven to 325° F.

2. Heat oil until very hot. Dry the meat pieces thoroughly. Add piece by piece to the hot oil to brown well.

3. When each piece has browned, season with the salt and black pepper.

4. Remove the meat and add all the large-cut vegetables (3 kinds). Shallow fry until also *just* browned.

5. Add tomato paste to vegetables, stir and cook over a medium-high heat until the tomato darkens to a moderate brown.

6. Replace the meat and stir in the beef stock. Add the herbs—tied

or in a muslin bag; add red grape juice and tea, cover the pan and cook in preheated oven for 1½ hours.

7. Remove the meat pieces and strain the cooking liquor. Discard the herbs and vegetables. Moisten the meat but take out just enough liquid to cook the small carrots and onions.

8. Toss the garnish vegetables in a little oil to bring out flavor, add stock and cover tightly. Boil for 15 minutes until *just* tender.

9. Add cooked vegetable garnish and cooking liquid to the beef, add the rice vinegar and bring the entire dish to the boil. Remove all fat.

10. Stir in the moistened arrowroot with great care so that neither meat nor vegetables are broken. Add more arrowroot only if necessary for a thicker sauce.

11. Scatter in the parsley, taste the sauce and adjust the seasoning. Sprinkle with 2 tablespoons rice vinegar; stir in gently.

12. Serve hot in an oval earthenware casserole.

(⑂) *"MINUTE STEAKS" can provide the answer*

The objective here was to select a beef steak that would give at least a 4-ounce serving and cover as large an area of the plate as possible for about 50¢ a serving.

Our selection was the *real* "London broil," a cut from the flank (an extension of the tail end of the T-bone). It is very lean and can be cooked and sliced diagonally or pre-sliced and fried individually. We feel it is best cooked whole. Having first "seasoned" it with an instant meat tenderizer as per the instructions, cook in a heavy skillet over moderate heat for about 2 minutes on either side; then carve it through diagonally. A *full* 1-pound piece will serve 4 people for an everyday meal (4 ounces of a complete protein food at night is enough). The lack of fat and bone makes it the same price as a beef chuck arm or shoulder steak selling for $1.39 per pound,° which can also be broiled —but these cuts are more fatty and don't "present" as well.

NUTRITION COMMENT. The flank steak is an excellent cut as seen by this profile (for 120 g. or 4 oz.): 252 calories (good); 41.1 g. protein (good); no carbohydrate (good); 8.32 g. fat (very good); B Vitamins (good). *Caution:* Some popular tenderizers have salt and dextrose added to the papain (tenderizer). This *could* be a problem to people on sodium-restricted diets.

° Prices at the time of writing.

BUDGET ADVANTAGE. Flank at $1.99 per pound costs 50¢ per 4-ounce serving. Hamburger at $1.00 per pound costs only 25¢ per 4-ounce serving, but regular hamburger contains approximately 22 percent fat. Flank has very little fat and looks much better, covering a larger area of the plate and thus providing great visual satisfaction.

So essentially it must be regarded as a "better buy" or more "value for your money" and that is what makes up the word "budget." Cheap food is a poor substitute for satisfaction because I view the available money as finance for good health and enjoyment, not for bulky dull fodder!

STEAK—cutting out the sinew adds so much

We look upon meat costs as one of the great burdens of our era, especially when such costs part us from our supersteaks. So you will find this technique especially important and well worth the little extra effort, to see that we get the maximum enjoyment from those occasional steaks. I'm talking about removing the small sinew found in almost all the back steaks that, if left in, contracts, hardens and can bend a thin steak out of all proportion. This causes parts of the steak to overcook and others to undercook. It's a lousy spectacle whichever way you look at it! So here is the way to "cut it out"!

SENSE ADVANTAGE is almost entirely visual but there are certain textural plus factors: removing the hard gristle and retaining greater juiciness.

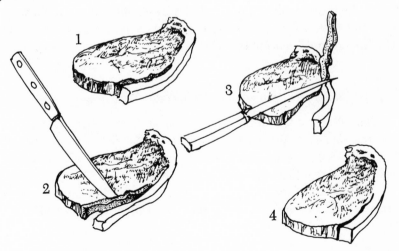

PAN-FRIED STEAK

Crush one clove of garlic and spread it over *four* New York strip steaks (each weighing about 6 to 7 ounces) which have had the sinew removed. Scrape it right off so that no shred of garlic fiber can be seen. Season with a *little* salt and ground black peppercorns. Heat a skillet and pan fry until browned on either side in sesame/safflower oil (see page 159). Serve with mushrooms (page 185) and watercress dipped in our *new* French Dressing (page 176).

(L) *SUPERCHUNK could mean a better stew for you!*

For stews and casseroles it is better to cut meat rich in connective tissue (such as beef chuck, lamb shoulder and neck, pork shoulder, veal shin) into large pieces, rather than the usually suggested 1-inch cube.

It is easier to do the initial browning because there are fewer pieces to turn, they cover less area on a restricted pan base and there are fewer exposed cut surfaces (i.e., a 6-ounce portion raw weight, cut into 2 large 3-ounce cubes, has 12 sides. Six 1-ounce cubes would have 36 sides). In addition, the connective tissue has a greater chance to dissolve through low moist heat transfer than does that in the smaller cubes which tighten by initial "shock" browning.

The best example of this technique is given on page 129 where we have created a "reformed" Boeuf Bourguignon that we call Napa Valley Casserole. It drastically reduces calories by eliminating the usual wine, flour and butter, yet manages (in our opinion) to *improve* the taste. The "superchunk" concept is vital to this dish.

(\$) *BRISKET, the thin edge of the wedge that works!*

This is one of the all time *great* meat buys, *but*—be careful to specify the *thin end*, also called "Straight Cut," "Flat Cut" or "Square Cut." This will give you *very little fat*, and for this idea to work you must have very little fat.

The thick or back end is very fatty and a poor buy unless *half the price* of the thin end. The new standard USDA term to look for is "beef brisket flat half, boneless."

The recipe used must be *moist* cookery and pot roast is excellent.

Budget advantage. We went out to check on the brisket business and discovered the following price range: *

Thick End	$1.49 to $1.89
Thin End	$1.30 to $1.79

In most stores we found that no distinction was made between thick and thin. The moral of this story is, if the cut is thin, buy it; if it's thick, *don't*—even if, as is the case with "specials," the thick end gets down to 75¢.

Nutritional advantage. Beef fat is saturated. We are on the warpath (in this book) against *excessive* consumption of total fats and this includes saturated fats. We therefore are consistent in asking you to not buy super fat cuts on special sale just in the *apparent* interests of economy!

POT ROAST BRISKET
(Serves 4)

1 large carrot	2 lbs. brisket
1 medium onion	Salt
1 clove garlic	Black pepper
1 pint beef stock	2 heaped tbsps. tomato paste
1 lb. long straight carrots	1 bay leaf
¼ cup polyunsaturated vegetable oil	¼ tsp. thyme

First prepare:

Peel and roughly chop the carrot and onion. Peel and squash the garlic. Measure beef stock. Preheat oven to 350° F. Peel the long carrots and leave whole.

Now cook!

1. Trim excess fat from the brisket (if any).

2. Heat a moderate-sized dutch oven—it should *just* provide enough room for the brisket. Add the oil and shallow-fry the vegetables and garlic.

3. Remove the vegetables and add the brisket; brown all over and season with salt and pepper.

* Prices at the time of writing.

4. Add the beef stock mixed with the tomato paste and the herbs.

5. Cover and allow to cook in the oven for 1½ hours (in some cases, 2 hours may be necessary—if the meat is "older" or has been working harder); at the end of this time turn the oven off and allow the meat to cool in the oven for 30 minutes.

6. Drain off the cooking juices and sieve the vegetables so that the pulp thickens the "sauce." Adjust the seasoning and replace the brisket to heat through on a very low heat in the same dutch oven on top of the stove.

7. Cut the carrots in quarters lengthwise, place in cold salted water, cover and bring to a boil. Boil for about 8 minutes or until *just* done.

8. Carve the brisket in the kitchen and lay overlapping slices on an oval dish. Cover with bubbling hot sauce and garnish with the long carrot sticks.

HOME-GROUND HAMBURGER gets the fat out!

As a simple test we purchased hamburger "freshly ground" straight from the counter, took it home and prepared it within 24 hours. It was greasy, fatty, had "off" tastes and cost 98¢ a pound—it wasn't worth it! So we decided to try several different cuts and grind them ourselves. We tried:

- Two parts beef chuck blade steak (at $1.09 per pound) to one part beef shank (at $1.19) = 72¢ + 39¢ = $1.11 per pound = 27¢ per person (1 pound serves 4).
- Beef flank steak (at $1.99) = $1.99 per pound = 49¢ per person.
- Two parts beef heel of round (at $1.39) to one part beef shank (at $1.19) = $1.31 per pound = 32¢ per person.*

Of the above, the flank gave an excellent product but the heel of round plus beef shank had more texture and flavor. This is therefore the top selection at $1.31 per pound or 32¢ per person against 24¢ for regular store-ground meat.

However, the big issue must be *taste* and whether or not you do your own grinding at home. We believe you can make an infinitely superior product that is worth the effort—especially considering the reduction in fat and calories.

NUTRITIONAL ADVANTAGE. Calorie value is reduced by using lean

---

* Prices at time of writing.

ground beef, and note that the protein goes UP. Some hamburgers contain 30 percent fat (the maximum permitted under law); thus my figures can get even "better." Note also that the higher the fat percentage the greater the shrinkage.

The following figures are for ¼ pound (4 ounces) of raw meat, when broiled:

	COOKED WEIGHT	CALORIES	PROTEIN	FAT
Regular (21.3% fat)	85 g.	224	21.8 g.	14.5 g.
Our mix (10% fat)	86 g.	140	25.9 g.	3.4 g.

(You *save* 84 calories per ¼-pound hamburger!)

SENSE ADVANTAGE can become a problem due to fat reduction. Fat equals flavor, therefore less fat equals less flavor. In order to remedy this, add, at the last moment, 1 teaspoonful of naturally brewed soy sauce per patty. The fat flavor is returned without fat! (See "Soy Sauce Versus Animal Fats" on page 156.)

We do get sense advantages in visual and aromatic areas. Ground beef is subject to rapid bacterial growth—the longer it is exposed to the air the more discolored (oxidized) it gets and the more it is potentially subject to off flavors.

EQUIPMENT needed is a very small hand-operated meat grinder costing about $13.50 at most good hardware stores.

⏱ HAMBURGER *with ice in the center!*

Here is a quick, easy and definitely unusual way to build some excitement and originality into the backyard burger! Simply dilute some soy sauce with an equal quantity of water and freeze it *solid* in a small ice cube tray. It's better if you can find a *ball-shaped* ice tray but not vital. Use unseasoned freshly ground hamburger (better if you grind it yourself in an old-fashioned meat grinder*). Weigh up 6 ounces, roll into a ball and spread out flat. Place the soy cube in the center, fold the meat about it, shape and broil as normal.

The ice will keep the fats from melting out and that keeps the flavor in—it will be juicier and more flavorsome than the usual ham-

---

* See above.

burger. You can adjust the soy content until, to *your* taste, it is only *just* there.

SENSE ADVANTAGE is in better texture, flavor, appearance and aroma.

NUTRITION COMMENT. There is an advantage *if* you grind your own beef and aim for a low fat content. You will find the soy sauce replaces the flavor lost when using less fat.

🪙 SOY BEANS *"extend"* meats to a degree

Much has been mentioned about soy extenders for hamburger, yet people's natural aversion to the use of *stretchers* has led to such cute statements as, "I'll eat half the meat and have my beans on the side." There are definite advantages to soy extenders *but* the taste factor *is* a real problem—or rather *was* a problem until now.

First let's look at the cost. One foil-packed job weighs in at 2.1 ounces and costs 29¢ (about $2.20 per pound).* Based upon the package directions you can expect a saving, which is easily computed as follows:

1 pkt. TVP† (weight ranges from 1.65 ounces at 25¢ to 2.1 ounces at 29¢) *added to*

1 lb. hamburger *plus*

⅔ cup water *gives*

—————

1½ lbs. meat—therefore your cost of ½ lb. meat equals the cost of the TVP pkt. plus flavoring. Thus if your meat costs you $1.00 per pound you stand to save between 14–17% per "extended" pound.

Try this mixture. Make up a 25 percent soy mix (i.e. ⅜ ounce—2 tablespoons—soy extender to 3 ounces hamburger). For 1 pound you will need four ounces of reconstituted TVP (8 level tablespoons—1½ ounces—of TVP mixed with 1 tablespoon soy sauce, 2 tablespoons of tomato ketchup and 2 tablespoons of water) and 12 ounces of meat. Allow 10 minutes for the TVP mix to rehydrate and *combine flavors*, then add to the beef, shape and cook immediately for 3 minutes on either side at medium low heat. Try the new kind against the regular—you'll be surprised!

Do it yourself. If TVP is added by the meat market, they cannot call the meat hamburger; thus they may not be controlled by the 30

—————

* Prices at the time of writing.
† Textured Vegetable Protein.

percent fat maximum and may add more fat than meat to "help" the flavor (and lower *their* costs).

BUDGET ADVANTAGE is very slight and frankly, if added in the normal package-direction manner, you will clearly taste the beans and the hamburger tastes like the bottom of a horse's feedbag on a wet day—but it does equal 14¢ to 17¢ potential saving per pound. Just multiply that by your hamburger use per year and it has real meaning. The technique offered by us does *not* represent a saving—it's break-even time—but we have begun to use a grain protein to replace, in part, an animal protein and this is where it's a valuable first step in an *essential walk* we must make to spread the available food to the four corners of the world.

SENSE CAUTION. Please note that we specify *immediately cooking the instant the TVP is added*. As each minute goes by the flavor deteriorates rapidly.

NUTRITIONAL ADVANTAGE. If TVP is added by the meat market they cannot call the meat mix "Hamburger," thus they are, *in some states,* relieved of the controlling law that specifies a maximum of 30 percent fat for "Hamburger." It is thus possible that TVP-extended hamburger *could* contain *more* fat in order to help the flavor and lower *their* costs but would have an adverse effect on *our* health. *Note:* New York State has issued a label regulation that TVP mixtures shall not contain more than 30 percent fat. You should check this out where you live.

💲 BRAINS *need some camouflage to find favor!*

Calves' brains are a good buy at about $1.50* a pound—that is, if you don't mind the idea. The thought from the cook's viewpoint can often be overcome but it's when the brains hit the plate that things start to go wrong! We have an idea you might like that avoids the limelight or at least manages to change the color!

Brains must first be soaked in cold water for a least 4 hours to dilute the residual blood. Rinse and trim off any discolored areas.

Place in cold water, bring slowly to the boil, drain and place in cold tap water to prevent overcooking. Dip into beaten egg and then in breadcrumbs and shallow-fry for 2 minutes on either side in sesame/safflower oil (p. 159). Serve with lemon.

And when they ask—just smile!

* Price at time of writing.

$(\$)$ *CUT UP and cook a 9-pound Shank End of Ham (smoked and cooked)*

Third and last of our "Cut Up and Cook" series. We now get cracking on a shank end of ham that produces 20 portions over 5 to 7 different meals at an average cost per serving of 36.8¢.*

CUTTING INSTRUCTIONS FOR HAM

1. Place ham with the cut end flat on cutting board as shown. Begin cut at the top or shank between the two end bones. Cut down, keeping the knife blade pressed against the bone to the left, all the while pulling away with the left hand. Portion A is the "kebob cut" and portion B is called the "cushion."

2. Here we show the cushion, B, with the skin being cut off (in very thin layers). Pieces C are the fat trimmings, which can be rendered. This is done by putting them in a little water and cooking at a gentle heat so that they melt out. Refrigerate and the fat comes to the top and then solidifies. Skim off and you'll have the same lard you'd pay 65¢ a pound for. Set skin aside.

3. The cushion is shown with the fat under skin trimmed off. Begin cut by inserting knife into natural seam as shown. As you cut into the seam, and down, pull away the curved portion, B-1, with your left hand.

4. B-1 is shown cut away from B-2. Now the gristle underpiece, B-3, is cut away from B-2, which is used for the Family Ham in Pajamas recipe.

5. Place B-1 with the rounded side on the board. Then cut as shown in cutlets half an inch thick. It will make four or five cutlets.

6. Here we are cutting out the bone on the kebob portion, A. As you cut along the bone, pull the meat back. This meat is cubed and used for the Ham Kebob recipe.

7. Here we have all the cuts assembled. On the left is the trimmed bone, D, from the kebob portion, used for stock. Next is the kebob meat, A, before and after it is cubed. The cutlets, B-1, are for the Ham Cutlet recipe. The family ham, B-2, is for Family Ham in Pajamas. B-3 is the

* Ham cost 79¢ per pound and weighed 9 pounds 5.12 ounces = $7.36—price at time of writing.

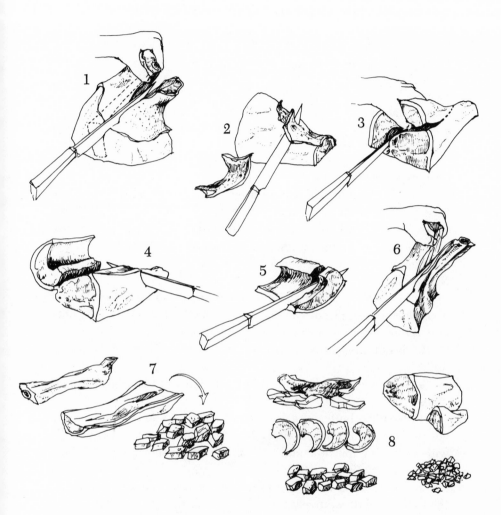

gristle underpiece, which is best used for flavoring soups or other dishes. The small diced meat E, is trimmings from throughout the ham and is used in the Open-Face Ham Omelet. F (the skin) is used for a super stock. And C is the fat which makes lard, as explained in instruction 2 above. Wrap each portion tightly in freezer wrap and refrigerate or freeze for future use.

Freezing. See page 121 for correct freezing technique.

Four simple recipes for the main cuts obtained are as follows:

OPEN-FACE HAM OMELET
(Serves 4)

1 cup (8 oz.) finely chopped
  ham pieces
8 eggs
2 tbsp. parsley
½ cup black olives
½ cup cooked potatoes

½ cup green peppers
½ cup tomato flesh
2 tsp. salt
2 tsp. ground white pepper
1 tbsp. butter

First prepare:

Soak the ham in cold water for one hour, drain and dry. Separate egg yolks from whites. Wash and chop parsley. Pit and chop the black olives. Dice the potatoes and green peppers. Skin tomatoes, remove seeds and cut into large pieces. Preheat broiler (see step 6 below). Use a frypan that can be placed under the broiler.

Now cook!

1. Shallow-fry the ham pieces in a dry pan, adding the green peppers, black olives, diced potatoes and parsley in that order. Toss until heated through, set to one side and add the tomato.

2. Season the egg yolks with salt and pepper and whip the whites stiffly.

3. Combine the yolks and whites as *lightly* but thoroughly as possible.

4. Melt the butter in a large omelet pan or non-stick skillet and heat until it *just* browns. Pour in the omelet mix and stir it vigorously with a fork (or spurtle) until the mix has coagulated (started to firm up—about 2 minutes).

5. Now mix in the filling previously cooked and kept warm—do this lightly and decoratively over the entire surface, like a pizza!

6. Place the whole pan with the omelet under the broiler to *set* the surface (60 seconds).

7. Slip the omelet from the pan onto a round serving dish and cut into pie-shaped wedges.

HAM CUTLETS
(*Serves 4*)

4 ham cutlets
2 tbsp. honey
2 bananas

2 tbsp. oil
½ cup fresh orange juice

First prepare:
Soak cutlets in cold water for one hour. Remove and dry thoroughly. Brush cutlets with honey. Skin bananas and slice the long way.
Now cook!
1. Place cutlets in preheated pan over a low heat. Cook 4 minutes on each side. Raise the heat to *just* brown the meat and remove to stainless steel platter.
2. Heat oil in the frying pan. Add bananas and cook one minute on each side, until just browned. Lay alongside cutlets on platter.
3. The honey, ham and banana residue can be scraped up in a little fresh orange juice at the boil and the reduced sauce poured over the cutlets as a glaze.

HAM KEBOBS
(*Serves 4*)

24 oz. cubed ham (24 pieces)
2 Golden Delicious apples
2 tbsp. lemon juice
1 green pepper

4 mushrooms
8 cherry tomatoes
4 tbsp. teriyaki sauce

First prepare:
Soak ham pieces in enough water to cover for one hour, then pour off and dry. Cut apples into 4 cubes each. Soak in lemon juice to keep from turning brown. Cut green pepper into 8 square-shaped chunks. Wash mushrooms and tomatoes.
Now cook!
Using four skewers, place ingredients in this order: ham, cherry tomato, ham, pepper, ham, cherry tomato, ham, apple, ham, apple,

pepper, ham. Place a mushroom on end of each skewer. Cook under or over grill 7 minutes on each side, brushing with teriyaki sauce the last 2 minutes on each side.

FAMILY HAM IN PAJAMAS
(Serves 7 or 8)

1 family ham (about 2½ lbs.)
1 tbsp. powdered cloves
1 tbsp. powdered mustard
1 egg yolk
¼ tsp. salt
2 tbsp. water

5-minute pastry:
8 tbsp. (1 stick) butter
1 cup all-purpose flour
Pinch of salt
½ cup ice water

First prepare:

Make pastry: Cut butter into small cubes and place in bowl with sifted flour. Shake to cover with flour. Add pinch of salt. Squeeze out each piece of butter into a thin sheet by pressing between forefinger and thumb, or use a pastry blender. Do this lightly and quickly. Add water all at once and stir into dough. Turn out onto floured board. Knead a few times, roll out, fold over once and chill for 20 minutes. Then roll and cut to size required.

Rub ham all over with powdered cloves and mustard. Wrap the ham with the pastry. Decorate it simply, with pastry leaves. Combine egg yolk with ¼ teaspoon salt and 2 tablespoons water; brush pastry with this gilding. Lay ham on rack in roasting pan.

Now cook!

1. Set oven at 425° F.; put ham in oven, watching it carefully. If some parts of pastry brown too quickly, cover those parts with aluminum foil.

2. Bake for approximately 25 minutes until the pastry has crusted and browned well.

3. Remove and serve while hot with normal ham accompaniments.

PORK CRACKLING—Superskin!

When anything is as good as this, there simply has to be a drawback! In this case it's the fat content of the skin and its double effect of saturated fat intake and calorie burden *but,* we have some *escapes* for you!

First, we must advise on the cut. You should *order* ahead of time from your meat supplier a *5-pound fresh ham shank, with the rind* (*heavy outer skin*) *left intact.* You will now have fresh pork from the lower hind leg with the skin on.

In order to get the crackling crisp you make ¼-inch deep incisions with a sharp knife every ¼ inch in hoops right about the leg (see illustration). Rub salt into these "scores" and baste well with the mixture given below. Roast at 375° F. for 25 minutes per pound until the internal temperature is 175° F. (see Meat Thermometers, page 123).

SENSE ADVANTAGE is clearly a visual one at first, but when the pieces are eaten they are delicate, crisp and full of flavor, an ideal foil for the smooth meat they cover.

NUTRITION COMMENT. A word of *caution* here. There is a danger of consuming too much fat by leaving the rind in place. To avoid this you *must* cut away the crackling from the underfat and then carve *all* the underfat away and remove it from the table. It should *not* be eaten. By doing this the small piece of crisp skin will not be out of balance with the normal fat-to-meat ratio.

BUDGET ADVANTAGE. This is a good, inexpensive roast. Look for it at about 70¢* per pound; it provides enough to serve 10 people at 35¢ per serving.

* Price at time of writing.

BASTE FOR ROAST PORK CRACKLING

Place ½ cup safflower oil in a small saucepan and add ½ teaspoon thyme, ½ teaspoon caraway seed, 2 cloves of garlic (crushed) and ¼ teaspoon salt. Cover and simmer slowly for 10 minutes; cool, strain and discard solids. Use the oil as a baste on roast pork to get the "crackling" crisp.

LAMB—should it be cooked "pink"?

I must warn you here that I may be guilty of prejudice. Even though I've prayed hard to be removed from my old ways, I still feel *strongly* that the French technique of roasted lamb *underdone* is absolutely wrong. It is *only* the young (immature) meat that is treated in this manner. However, I feel we should go up to and *just beyond the pink stage*, that is, until the juices turn colorless. In this way we sidestep the slippery plastic taste so often associated with undercooked "young" meat.

I strongly suggest that you buy a meat thermometer—they cost about $6–$7* for a good one (see page 123)—and roast to an internal temperature of 155° F.

SENSE ADVANTAGE is a textural one: the meat is crisp yet not slippery, it is full of moisture and flavor. Because of the "moisture" being *cooked* you get a full aroma, not a partly stale ammonia smell.

NUTRITIONAL COMMENT. We do not "lose" B vitamins (niacin, thiamine) due to "overcooking." The "loss" that is experienced would be lost in juices in any event. However, be sure that you do not exceed the 155° mark by much as then the losses can be relatively heavy. FOR A SIMPLE LEG OF LAMB, slide one garlic clove up into the meat close to the bone, at least five inches up from the shank end. Rub seasoned (salt and white pepper) flour into the fat surface and slash the fat in places where it is thick. Place in a 350° F. oven and roast for 30 minutes per pound until the meat thermometer reads 155° F. Carve and serve with red currant jelly or a light onion sauce.

* Prices at time of writing.

⊙ *NEW ZEALAND LAMB is wonderful when "matured"*

A really important contribution can be made to our domestic budgets by shopping for New Zealand lamb. You are going to have to be insistent, because lamb just isn't that popular. The reason is the high price of our locally reared animals coupled with an old hang-up about imported frozen lamb being tough, tasteless and having an odd smell.

According to my information, New Zealand lamb has only *once* in 10 years exceeded the price of local lamb. It is also a *very good* buy relative to other protein foods at this time. As for the flavor problem, it's interesting that this problem has been overcome for *our* market. In New Zealand, they are now "maturing" the lambs after slaughter before they freeze them. In the old days they were frozen soon after they were killed and the excessive moisture caused "odd" aromas.

Notwithstanding their action, however, I *always* defrost all imported lamb and "hang" it by an S-shaped butcher's hook from the refrigerator rungs for 3 days before cooking. I wipe it over with a vinegar-soaked piece of cheesecloth each day and keep it under refrigeration. The result is perfect, every time.

FLAVOR ADVANTAGE is increased, with great tenderness, and the ammonia smell is gone.

ROAST LEG OF LAMB NELSON
(*Serves 6 to 8*)

*1 4-lb. leg of lamb—wipe dry
with a clean cloth
1 tbsp. flour, sifted and seasoned
with salt and white pepper*

*6 sprays parsley, very fresh and
well washed
1 10-oz. can apple and orange
juice, opened and placed in a
small saucepan**

Method:

1. Rub the lamb with the seasoned flour and shake off any surplus.

2. Make several even and decorative shallow incisions in the heavy outer fat layers and pack into these some well-washed pieces of parsley.

* If you cannot find apple/orange mixed, simply combine 5 fluid ounces (⅝ cup) each of orange juice and clear apple juice.

(If you have some marjoram it also gives a delightful flavor to lamb, but it must be used very sparingly.)

3. Preheat your oven to 325° F. and place the leg fat side uppermost on the cleaned rungs of your oven shelf; place the drip pan on the next shelf down. This is used to collect the drippings and to roast root vegetables if you wish to add them.

4. After 10 minutes of cookery draw out the top oven shelves so that the joint is exposed and place another drip pan immediately underneath the joint; now baste the leg with the apple and orange juice. The pan immediately below the leg will collect the surplus fruit juice and will save the vegetables from becoming saturated. Allow 30 minutes per pound of meat and baste with the juice at least four times during cooking.

5. When the joint is cooked, remove the vegetables, boil down the juice to ¼–⅓ cup and spoon the syrupy mixture over the joint, having raised the temperature of the oven to 500° F. This high heat will form a crisp golden orange and apple glaze on your lamb in 5 to 10 minutes which is as delicious as it is attractive. The balance of the fruit juice can be added to the meat drippings in the vegetable pan, to form a fruit gravy.

😊 *LAMB'S KIDNEYS can be refreshed*

A somewhat stale lamb's kidney can be one of those experiences that get one "off-track" with almost all variety meats for the rest of one's life! But all is not lost, there is a way to bring them back to a stage when the senses can applaud their return!

Prepare the kidney by removing all the surrounding fat, then peel off the pale bluish skin and cut almost in half from the indented side. Remove the heavy veins and drive toothpicks through the lobes to hold them open and flat.

Heat 2 tablespoons sesame/safflower oil in a frypan. Place kidneys in the pan so that the cut surface is uppermost and fry briskly for 2 minutes. Turn them over for a few seconds and then turn out onto a paper towel to cool.

Blot dry and then reheat gently in the frypan (so as not to overcook). All those "off flavors" will be gone.

SENSE ADVANTAGE is largely an aromatic one—the ammonia smell is clearly destroyed. There is a slight reduction in juiciness.

Nutritional content. Kidneys are an excellent food—just look at this for a 3½-ounce (100-gram) lamb's kidney: 105 calories (good); 16.8 g. protein (good); 3.3 g. fat (good); and high in Vitamin A and in B Vitamins.

KIDNEY CASSEROLE

Cook some small pork sausages and make up a combined dish with chopped bacon, mushrooms, baby onions and the kidneys (but remember—don't ever overcook the kidneys). You can tie these ingredients together with a simple brown sauce, ¼ cup red grape juice, 1 teaspoon rice vinegar, and ½ teaspoon cold unsweetened tea.

Pastry

😊 *PASTRY must relax before it is cut*

Any form of pastry that needs to be rolled out must *relax* before it's used and trimmed. It is strange that this simple rule isn't used in more basic cookbooks. The facts are that when the pastry has been "stretched," it will hold itself in that shape while it is raw but, when subjected to heat, soon retreats with indecent speed. When the pastry is placed on top of a pie, its "retreat" is painfully obvious!

Just leave the pastry in its rolled-out form for 10 minutes at room temperature and you've got it made—quite literally, it will have relaxed!

SENSE ADVANTAGE is one of visual benefit. One of the most obvious tests is the pastry top used on a treacle tart (see recipe below).

TREACLE TART

For a treacle tart that Her Majesty, Queen Elizabeth, the Queen of England, likes very much (so I was told second-hand!) you will need, for 10 servings:

Pastry to line tart:
1½ cups self-rising flour
6 tbsp. (¾ stick) butter
¼ cup milk
½ egg
Pinch of freshly ground salt

Top pastry:
8 tbsp. (1 stick) butter
¼ cup sugar
1½ eggs
1½ cups self-rising flour
2 tsp. sugar

148

Filling:
16 fl. oz. (1 pt.) Tate & Lyle's
  golden syrup (or use a thick
  light corn syrup)
5 oz. fresh white bread crumbs

First prepare:

Make bottom pastry by mixing butter lightly into sifted flour and then stirring into a dough with milk, half an egg and salt. (To divide egg in half beat lightly first.) Knead lightly, refrigerate 30 minutes.

Make top pastry by creaming butter with sugar, adding half an egg, beaten, and, when thoroughly mixed, folding in the sifted flour. Refrigerate. Lightly beat remaining egg.

Measure golden syrup. Make bread into 1¼ cups. Preheat oven to 375° F.

Now cook!

1. Roll out bottom pastry on a floured surface to an 11-inch circle; leave for 10 minutes to "relax." Line a 9-inch flan ring standing on a greased tray. Trim off pastry and prick base with a fork.

2. Combine bread crumbs with golden syrup and fill pastry case.

3. Roll out top pastry or press out with hands to a 9-inch round on a well-floured board. Roll lightly with rolling pin and then turn it over and again allow to "relax."

4. Brush rim of tart with beaten egg and then place pastry top onto tart. Press edges together and trim off any excess pastry. Crimp edges and brush surface with beaten egg. Prick surface with a fork. Sprinkle with sugar and bake in oven for 20 minutes. Remove and allow to cool.

Service:

The tart must first cool for an hour. It can then be reheated at 250° F. for 5 minutes. Whipped cream goes well on the side—but then, so does yoghurt. (Please note that this is a dish highly suited to one who needs to *increase* weight!)

PASTRY PIES *without a soggy bottom!*

Many pies and tarts, flans, quiche—call them what you may—suffer from soggy bottoms. All manner of techniques have been developed to deal with them but two seem worthy of attention.

The first—to be used only for sweet pastries—is apricot jam melted and brushed lukewarm over the partly cooked pastry base.

The second is to use an egg wash, made up of 1 whole egg, ½ teaspoon salt and 1 tablespoon light salad oil. This is completely combined and brushed over the precooked pastry case and then filled.

SENSE ADVANTAGE is primarily a textural one but clearly there is a benefit to the digestion (at least in my case).

APPLE CUSTARD TART
(Serves 6)

Pastry:
1 cup flour
Pinch salt
1 tbsp. sugar
4 tbsp. (½ stick) butter
1 egg, separated
3 drops vanilla extract
Water

Filling:
¼ cup instant milk powder
1 cup applesauce
3 eggs
1 tsp. vanilla extract
1 tsp. grated lemond rind
1 cup regular milk
Nutmeg

Method:

1. Combine flour, salt and sugar. Cut in butter. Stir in egg yolk, vanilla and enough cold water to form pastry into a ball. Press into 9-inch pie plate lined with foil. Bake at 375° F. for 12 minutes. Remove from oven and while hot brush with "egg wash" (see above).

2. Combine instant milk powder, applesauce, eggs, vanilla and lemon rind. Gradually beat in milk. Pour apple custard mixture into partially baked shell. Grate a little nutmeg over surface. Bake at 325° F. for 50 minutes. Serve cold.

CUSTARD PIES need two lots of "custard"

Many attempts at such dishes as Pumpkin Pie and Quiche Lorraine are doomed to failure because of the "one-hit" filling technique where all the mix is added at one time and the pie is carried with trembling hands to the oven. The filling expands as it heats and pours over the lip of the pie plate.

All you have to do to avoid this is to place the pastry-lined pie plate or mold (filled with any non-liquid garnish) on the oven shelf and then add *half* the liquid. Put to bake at 400° F. for 2 minutes, then add the rest—taking care to leave a ¼-inch clearance from "custard" to top edge of pastry (which shrinks!).

NUTRITIONAL BENEFIT is found from making possible a new variety of easily prepared low-cost high-protein open pies such as Quiche Lorraine (per slice): 570 calories; 15.5 g. protein; 32.2 g. carbohydrate; 41.8 g. fat. The fat can be reduced by replacing the bacon with lean ham, thinly sliced.

SENSE ADVANTAGE. This method provides good visual appearance and helps to keep the base free from "sog" (see also page 150) which occurs because the overfilled mix can boil up to the rim and float underneath.

QUICHE LORRAINE
(*Serves 6*)

Pastry:
2 cups all-purpose flour
½ tsp. salt
8 tbsp. (1 stick) butter
1 small egg
1½ tbsp. ice water

Filling:
6 oz. bacon slices
3 oz. Gruyère cheese
3 eggs
1½ cups milk
Freshly ground salt
Freshly ground pepper
Nutmeg

First prepare:

Pastry: Sift flour with salt, form a well in center and add softened butter and egg. Mix gently with fingertips. Stir in ice water until soft dough is formed. Knead dough a few times into a ball. Refrigerate 30 minutes. Roll out pastry and put in an 8-inch pie plate, fluting a high edge on pastry shell. Prick bottom with a fork. Place a piece of cheese-cloth over the bottom and sides of pastry. Fill with dried peas and bake in 425° F. oven for 20 minutes. Remove cheesecloth and dried peas and allow to cool.

Filling: Lightly fry bacon and cut into strips to fit pastry bottom.

Cut cheese into thin slices. Mix eggs with milk and season with salt, pepper and nutmeg. Preheat oven to 400° F.

Now cook!

1. Place bacon strips on bottom of pastry shell. Sprinkle with thin slices of Gruyère cheese. Put on oven shelf. Pour over half of the milk and egg mixture, leave in the hot oven for 2 minutes to set and then add remaining liquid.

2. Bake for 25 to 30 minutes. Remove from oven, place on serving dish and serve hot or cold, cut into small wedges.

Special hints: You can use bread crusts in lieu of peas. Allow a ¼-inch clearance between egg and milk mixture and the pastry shell lip.

THE ROLLING PIN *that thinks for itself!*

There is a pretty general problem experienced by new cooks and "old" cooks alike: a difficulty in gauging the thickness or thinness of a sheet of pastry.

Some dishes, such as the French Vol au Vent (a pastry case made from puffed pastry), call for the pastry to be ¼-inch to ⅜-inch thick, while some pies specify ⅛ inch and some recipes even go down to nearly "zero" for pasta.

The experts simply run their fingers under the edge and "feel" the distance with their thumbs. Now we have a wooden rolling pin based on a French design that has round rolling discs at each end that raise or lower the rolling surface of the pin at will. It works.

¼6″ ⅛″ ¼″

EASY TO ADJUST;
REMOVE ENDS AND INSERT INTERCHANGEABLE DISCS

NUTRITION COMMENT relates to the whole pastry business. Did you know that pastry made with 6 ounces of butter and 1 pound of flour looks like this: 3,034 calories; 53.7 g. protein; 381.7 g. carbohydrates; 142.2 g. fat!

That's enough to make me want to think of another method. So I looked at the possibility of making a hollowed-out breadcase (use the crumbs for breading purposes). One case equals about 3 slices of white bread.

	WEIGHT	CALO-RIES	PROTEIN	FAT	CARBOHY-DRATES
Breadcase	75 grams	210	6 grams	3 grams	13 grams
Vol au Vent Case	75 grams	433	7.6 grams	20.3 grams	54.5 grams

On face value it looks like a clean sweep for bread!

To make the breadcase cut a superthick slice from a whole loaf (unsliced) measuring 3 inches wide:

1. Cut down into the bread keeping the incisions ½ inch in from the crust. Cut down to within ½ inch of the base.

2. Now slice off the browned outer crusts carefully.

3. Pinch and tear out the dough center, then bake in a 200° F. oven until hard but not colored.

Seasonings and Oils

☺ *TOMATO PASTE is one of the most exciting seasoning products I buy*

I do not know quite how I could function as a cook without a good thick tomato paste. Much of my cooking is vivid in flavor, with deep, rich colors, and this is precisely what tomato paste provides.

I use it as a deep coloring by adding it after the meat has been browned. The paste is stirred into the *frying* dish and cooked until it goes through a deep red into almost a dark brown color. The cooking liquid (stock, etc.) can then be added and the whole dish looks fabulous. What happens is that the heat hastens the non-enzymatic browning which occurs in tomato products and with its color change comes a decided flavor change that imparts a strong and highly acceptable finish.

SENSE ADVANTAGE is visual, aromatic, taste and even textural—a "grand slam" of the senses.

NUTRITION COMMENT comes from Best and Taylor:

> Edible substances which are the most palatable or arouse the sensation of taste with the greatest intensity are the most potent salivary stimulants. . . . The main functions of saliva are to moisten and lubricate food which aids in digestion and to provide a protective secretion in the mouth, thus keeping mucous membranes moist and aiding in oral hygiene.*

* Charles H. Best and Norman B. Taylor, *The Physiological Basis of Medical Practice* (Baltimore, Md.: Williams & Wilkins, 1966).

In other words, whatever makes *your* mouth water can probably be better digested.

IDAHO CHILI PIE

4 large potatoes
Salt
18 oz. ground beef
1 clove garlic
1 medium onion (2 oz.)
¼ cup soy sauce with ¾ cup water
1 tbsp. safflower oil

2 oz. (¼ cup) tomato paste
3 tsp. ground chili powder
1 tsp. oregano
2 tbsp. butter
White pepper
1 tbsp. chopped parsley

First prepare:

Scrub potatoes and roll in salt. Weigh ground beef. Peel and crush garlic. Peel and finely chop onion. Mix the soy sauce and water. Measure remaining ingredients.

Now cook!

1. Place salted potatoes in an oven set at 350° F. for 1 hour 15 minutes until *just* starting to soften—don't overcook!

2. Cut a long, thin, even (¼-inch) slice off the top to form an "open boat" shape. Scrape out most of the flesh but leave about ¼ inch secured to the sides and bottom. Set aside and cover.

3. Fry the crushed garlic and the chopped onion in the safflower oil. Add the ground beef and fry until the meat separates, *drain excess fat from the pan*, then add the tomato paste and cook until it browns.

4. When a good, even dark brown color is achieved, sprinkle in 2 teaspoons chili powder (adding more if your tongue is asbestos!).

5. Add the soy sauce-water mixture and stir well. Cover, reduce the heat to low and simmer for 30 minutes. When the meat is cooked, add the oregano.

6. During the 30 minutes' simmering, take the potato flesh removed from the "boats" and whip this with a teaspoon chili powder, the butter and some salt and white pepper. Place it into a piping bag with a half-inch fancy star nozzle, if available.

7. Place the boats onto a white oval serving platter. Spoon the cooked chili mixture into them and pipe a good layer of potato decoratively on top (or spoon it on and mark the top with a fork).

8. Return the dish to the oven for 10 minutes to heat through, then brown the top under the broiler. Serve super-hot, dusted with chopped parsley.

SOY SAUCE versus animal fats

Cooking is, to say the least, an inexact science. If it were more exact a great deal of the emotion would be lost and the *need to cook* might be removed.

But we do know that an *excess* of certain foods can be bad. Too much animal fat, too much sugar and too much salt are well known examples. Therefore, when a chance comes to reduce fat and salt at one hit, it looks like a winner. We have experimented and are now convinced that fat can be reduced in traditionally high-fat dishes and replaced by a dash of naturally brewed soy sauce.

NUTRITIONAL ADVANTAGE. Reduction of both animal fat and salt is first-rate "reforming" of our excessive *misuse* of food. In one pound of regular hamburger there is usually about 3 ounces of fat (600 calories) that can be removed. This is all saturated fat, and while we need about 33 percent of our calories to be fat calories, the fact is that we get an "average" of 40 percent and in many cases as much as 50 percent from fats. This national average *might* include *us*, so it's reasonable to look for ways to reduce the impact. The salt consumption is also a grave problem. We *need* about ¼ teaspoon of sodium per day. Just imagine how much we get in processed foods that rely upon large salt doses to "lift" their otherwise bland products! And when all the salted potato chips and olives and crackers are done with, we pick up that salt at the table and lay it right on *without tasting*. This form of addiction can kill. In northern Japan, where huge quantities of salt (in excess of 30 pounds per year per man, woman and child) are consumed, the "stroke" rate is reported as the highest anywhere in the world. Salt is also said to harden the arteries. Our average need is ¼ teaspoon sodium per day so let's try to reduce our intake. On this point there is a special soy sauce made by Kikkoman with an 8 percent salt content—you may wish to taste it. Most other commonly found natural soy sauces have a 16 percent salt content.

SENSE ADVANTAGE comes from taste and aroma and color (in dark dishes). Soy sauce has been used by Zen Buddhists for generations to replace the animal fat forbidden by their religion. It does work. To test this theory, fry 1 pound of regular store-bought hamburger in 1 teaspoonful of sesame/safflower oil (page 159) over a medium heat; keep stirring to release the fat. Pour off the fat (should be about 3 ounces) and add 2 tablespoons naturally brewed soy sauce. Stir in and cook lightly. Combine with 1 cup of cooked rice (pages 202–03) and ¼ cup of *just* cooked green peas. Simple and delicious. You cut out the fat but retain the flavor.

CLARIFIED BUTTER *still has its place*

Butter burns at about 200° F. unless it is "clarified." The easiest method is to place 1 pound of butter in a small saucepan on a low heat; leave for 10 minutes, until a foam has risen to the top. Skim this off and place in a bowl. Pour the clear "butter oil" into a glass jar—this is "clarified butter." Place both containers, covered, in the refrigerator. The clarified butter will keep for about 5 weeks.

Add the sediment dregs to the "foam" and use for buttered vegetables. The clarified butter will fry foods in a temperature as high as 475° F., at least the equal of oil.

SENSE ADVANTAGE comes almost entirely from aroma; there is some flavor, but discernible only when used in large quantity—and then it has some obvious nutritional problems.

NUTRITION COMMENT. I'm concerned enough to give you a word of *Caution* here. I'm no longer convinced that saturated animal fats are harmless; neither, for that matter, am I yet convinced that hydrogenated margarines are harmless—but I do believe that correctly processed polyunsaturated vegetable oils can provide the *least* harmful means of culinary frying. There are, however, some foods—such as mushrooms—that cannot be prepared with oils or margarines as well as they can with butter. There is, therefore, a place for a *frying-temperature butter,* but please be *very* sparing in its use.

DEEP FRYING—*some efforts to reduce the adverse effects*

Deep frying is a technique that is not exactly high on the list of nutritional techniques, yet it does have *extremely high appeal* for the taste and we *can* minimize the *adverse aspects.*

Enemy No. 1 is type of fat. Animal fats, rendered beef suet and fat trim, must be among the worst "saturated" fats, yet when relatively fresh they are among the best for flavor. They are also cheaper and last longer than most commercial solid fats.

Enemy No. 2 is the temperature. It must be about 340° F. to 385° F. Too low and the fat is *absorbed* by the article, too high and the fat will be destroyed and loose its ability to fry quickly. Use a special thermometer, but heat the bulb first in warm water.

Enemy No. 3 is lack of cleanliness. Regardless of the use, the oil must be cleaned each time and kept *skimmed* with a flat wire skimmer during cooking. The greater the proportion of fine particles in the fat, the lower the "smoke" point; the lower the "smoke" point, the lower the temperature used for frying. The lower the temperature, the higher the fat absorption, and this spells T-R-O-U-B-L-E!—so keep it clean and *hot*.

NUTRITIONAL ADVANTAGES. The chief factors governing the amount of fat absorbed during frying are (1) time and temperature of cooking, (2) total cooking surface area of food, (3) composition and nature of food, (4) variation in smoking temperature of fat used.*

To take a specific case, frying in beef fat as compared with an oil such as safflower oil would mean greater fat absorption due to the lower temperature of frying necessary for the beef fat and the increased cooking time. There is also an overall increase in saturated fats over using a good polyunsaturated vegetable oil.

SENSE ADVANTAGE is improved by the clean, sweet taste that results from well-kept fat.

RECIPES. I would prefer not to recommend additional recipes to you but would refer you to Squash Chips (page 192) and French Fries (page 193), in which we have tried sincerely to reduce adverse nutritional body impact.

(\$) *HOME-SEASONED OIL puts your food in a different light*

Since the frying pan or skillet is, in our Western culture, the most-used piece of culinary equipment, it follows that we should have some kind of attitude towards the shallow-frying "oil."

* Pauline C. Paul *et al.,* eds., *Food Theory and Applications* (New York: John Wiley & Sons, 1972).

As a *standard*, we have suggested 1 part sesame seed oil to 20 parts of safflower oil—but how about a real "house oil," special to your home and personal likes. I tried one that has worked so well we are almost addicted to the taste! To each cup of safflower oil, add 2 large cloves fresh garlic (crushed), 1 teaspoon rosemary and 1 teaspoon oregano. Simmer together, without blackening the herbs, for 10 minutes with lid on. Cool, then strain carefully and bottle. Use this with fish, chicken or steak. It's a wonderful general seasoning all your very own!

We prefer standard processed sesame seed oil to that referred to as "cold pressed." The impact of severe heat upon certain nutritive elements of oil bearing seeds has been determined, as has been the effect upon the seeds of cold pressing. The process of cold pressing does involve very high heats, high enough to scorch the residue. For my part, I see the potential spoilage of cold pressed, coupled with its higher cost, as edging out the slight nutritive advantage.

ⓈGARLIC *can be a crushing experience!*

We shall assume that you believe that a fresh clove of garlic is better than all the dehydrated pieces, pastes and oils, etc., on the market today. Thus we can move on to consider how it should be crushed. Let's look at the alternatives.

1. *Garlic crusher*—forces clove through a fine mesh surface in a pulp. Good for distribution, but needs careful cleaning to remove stale odors.

2. *Scrape with salt*—messy and gets up your nails and over your hands; also anything that adds more salt to our diet is suspect!

3. *Pound in mortar*—produces good pulp; more easily cleaned than the *crusher*.

4. *Knife blade*—very quick. Inclined to "spurt" from under the blade and of course taint the board. To make it easier, use foil first as a "wrap around" the garlic clove and smash it with a blade. Then pass the blade over it in a light chopping motion. This is the least wasteful method, the easiest done without added purchase *but* that pestle and mortar is a wonderful thing to own!

⏱ GARLIC *can be peeled by the "pound"*

Garlic can best be purchased fresh and firm by the quarter pound and peeled all at one time with two simple knife cuts in each clove. Place the cloves in a wide-mouthed glass jar with a cork stopper under a light sesame/safflower oil (page 159).

The oil will seal the air from the garlic and keep it fit to use without refrigeration for up to 6 weeks. Flavor loss will occur if the cloves turn pale brown.

The external peeling leaves can be used to flavor cooking liquid for rice and pasta. Just bring the peel to the boil, then strain and use the clear flavored water to cook the pasta!

P.S. You can use the garlic-flavored oil in many of our dishes—you need only keep on topping it up.

☺ VEGETABLE *flavor oils*

Root vegetables and vegetables with a high degree of volatile oils, such as celery, will "give up" these oils when heated. At moist heat temperatures up to and including boiling point a degree of "release" takes place, but at a *frying* heat of 320° F. the flavor generation is much greater. The old "Professional Chef Schools" talk about "sweating off" the vegetables; the word "sweat" describes beads of volatile oils that are driven to the surface by the heat and exploded as aroma. We have focused on an interesting point here: if good flavor release is achieved, do we need less root vegetables as a flavor base? Normally roughly 1 pound of vegetables is used for 2 pounds of meat. In our test we reduced vegetables to 10 ounces (6 ounces saved) with no real flavor loss. The initial root vegetable base is thrown away in our stews and casseroles.

One way of testing this on your family is to shallow-fry some root vegetables instead of just boiling them (see the recipe given below). If that works, then I would urgently suggest you consider frying or "sweating off" all your root vegetables used in casseroles and stews.

SENSE ADVANTAGE. This method gives excellent flavor and aroma plus factors to all casseroles, stews and sauces. In fact, I find it an indispensable step in the correct use of vegetables.

LOW-MOISTURE VEGETABLE COOKERY

1. One pound of root vegetables, if carefully peeled, usually serves 4 people. I like to mix roots. My favorite combination is sweet potato, parsnip (with center core removed) and tender juicy carrots. If you have space *always* keep them in the refrigerator and cut them immediately before cookery. *Don't* cut and leave in cold water. Keep the peelings for soups.

2. Shallow-fry the root vegetables very gently in sesame/safflower oil (page 159) in a frypan with a close-fitting lid. Stir from time to time to keep from scorching.

(☺) *BOUQUET GARNI is really just a bunch of herbs*

Aromatic herbs give up their natural volatile oils to the sauces or liquids in which meats, poultry and sometimes seafood are cooked.

There is a "classical" bundle that includes—*almost without thought* —bay leaf, thyme, parsley, a piece of celery. Exactly why the culinary profession has bowed down to this singular lack of imagination is hard to understand unless it be their convenience in the sprig form (they are usually available fresh or dried, in the leaf or on the sprig). Tied in a bundle they can be removed before service; if only dried is available, then they can be crumbled up and placed in a piece of muslin, securely tied and dropped in. Whatever or whichever—the truth is that, by its addition, the average casserole or stew ceases to be average!

Variations can be made by adding marjoram or rosemary or dillweed for beef, lamb and pork respectively; the choice and opportunity are really yours, and it's *wide* open for initiative—so try today, won't you?

SENSE ADVANTAGE is primarily aromatic with perhaps a small taste "fringe benefit." Try to see it as an *infusion* of herbs—it works better that way.

BUDGET BENEFIT comes from its use with low-cost foods that need some sparkle.

NAVARIN OF LAMB

1 tbsp. sesame/safflower oil (page 159)

2 lbs. mutton shoulder meat, as lean as possible, cut into 2-inch pieces

Salt

Freshly ground black peppercorns

4 cloves garlic, well crushed

1 tbsp. sugar

½ cup red grape juice, 1 tsp. cold tea and 2 tsp. rice vinegar

½ pint lamb or veal stock (see page 171)

4 black peppercorns, 4 parsley stalks, ½ tsp. each rosemary and thyme, 2 bay leaves, placed in a muslin bag

12 whole small onions (pickling size)

1 tsp. sugar

12 small potatoes (all the same size), peeled

1 tbsp. chopped parsley

Method:

1. Pour oil into a heavy-based saucepan and add the shoulder meat; season in the pan with salt and ground black peppercorns and brown.

2. Add garlic when the meat has become a little brown; add also at this time a level tablespoon of sugar. Continue to cook until the sugar darkens.

3. Add the grape juice and tea and sufficient stock to just cover the meat and pop in the Bouquet Garni (bunch of herbs). Cover the pan and simmer for one hour.

4. Shallow-fry the onions in a little oil and add a teaspoonful of sugar to give them a deep golden brown color.

5. When the first hour of cookery is up, remove the herbs and add the onions and the small potatoes; add some more stock to just cover all these ingredients, replace the lid and simmer for another 30 minutes until the potatoes are cooked.

6. Skim the surface of any surplus fat, add 2 teaspoons rice vinegar, pour off the liquid and thicken with arrowroot (see page 167 for the technique), dust with chopped parsley and serve.

PARSLEY STALKS have more flavor than meets the eye!

If you have ever "grazed" through a bed of parsley it may have occurred to you that the decorative "head" has less flavor than the stalk. From that moment it doesn't take long to consider how to use the stalk as yet another seasoning—with a little "texture" thrown in.

I use the stalks finely chopped, ⅛ inch long, in sauces. When they are added 5 minutes before serving they retain their color and crispness. A few stalks, finely chopped, can also be used in omelets, scrambled eggs, crepes, batters, soufflés and gravies to great advantage.

Bunches of stalks give good flavor in casseroles, soups and stews and are easier to remove than clumps of soggy flowering heads.

SENSE ADVANTAGE is both textural and taste plus a fringe visual factor because most folk just can't work out what "they" are!

HOCK STOCK is nectar for vegetables

Small ham hocks weighing about 10 ounces (variously called "country ham hocks" or smoked pork hocks) are *not* a good buy—especially if taken from the *hind shank*. They are almost all bone and fat and hardly any meat. Ask for fore shanks and have them cut so that you get sufficient meat to cut for casserole and omelet uses (less expensive and better flavored, and less fatty than bacon). The bones give an excellent flavor, especially good for One Dish Vegetable Meals (see pages 193–97)—which are great ways to beat the budget!

You simply use the normal vegetable trimmings—celery tops, carrot and onion peels are all very good—strip back the skin from the hock (which helps speed the cooking time), cut off the meat for casserole use and add a bay leaf and some thyme, *no* salt. Simmer slowly for 1 to

2 hours. Two knuckles will make 1½ pints (24 fluid ounces) of finished, skimmed and strained stock of excellent quality.

For general method of use see Napa Valley Casserole on page 129.

😊 *LEMON is wonderful providing . . .*

Yes, lemons are fabulous, providing two vital things are always remembered.

The first is the shape of the lemon piece provided. If it is sliced into a thin decorative ring it is a useless waste of money. You can't squeeze it or eat it effectively! A lemon should be cut in wedges that can be squeezed. That is, the ends have to be trimmed first to provide a flat surface. I use a fork to jab into the quarter in order to release some of the juice without a struggle. Some restaurants tie a piece of cheesecloth around the half lemon to act as a pip restrainer and whilst that is fine for them, I feel it's a bit much for the home!

The other point is that if you are right-handed, you should squeeze the lemon with your left hand. The lemon skin is filled with volatile oils that spray back onto your hand and make it impossible to drink anything without a new "lemon fresh" aroma!

SENSE ADVANTAGE comes from cutting down on unwanted aromas and putting the flavor where it is needed.

💲 *CHEESE tastes better close to home*

And now here we are with a good, tangible saving that also delivers on the emotional front: the purchase of a good local Parmesan in its dry "block" condition as against the local or imported pregrated and packaged variety. Our costs indicated: *

| Local bulk | $3.04 per lb. | = | 19¢ per oz. |
| In a Glass Jar (Pregrated) | 95¢ per 2½ oz. | = | 38¢ per oz. |

However, if you buy *imported* from a good store:

| Bulk | $4.00 per lb. | = | 25¢ per oz. |
| In a Carton (Pregrated) | $2.95 per 12 oz. | = | 25¢ per oz. |

* Prices at time of writing.

But—you will have heavy rind on the bulk; on the other hand you will get a stale soapy taste with the pregrated. All in all we found the local bulk Parmesan best at 19¢ per ounce, with imported bulk at 25¢ per ounce a close runner-up. The worst buy for price and flavor was the local grated at 38¢ per ounce—it tastes awful!!

BUDGET ADVANTAGE. If you use ¼ pound of cooking cheese a week and buy the pregrated local cheese in 2½-ounce jars (it is widely sold) then you could save about $39 a year by buying the local bulk from a good food store.

EFFORT ADVANTAGE. Suggest you use either a small rotary hand grater available in all good gourmet departments, or a plain metal grater which is cheap and works very well if you watch your fingers!

OTHER IDEAS. Add it to pasta, such as spaghetti (see page 206); use over Baked Potatoes (page 201); put it on Filled Crêpes (pages 88–89). Or improve a mixed vegetable soup by adding fresh grated cheese. Just grate it right in—the taste addition is fantastic.

Sauces and Liquids

🌹 *ARROWROOT is a super thickener*

Sauces that require a mixture of equal parts of flour and butter combined and cooked (called a roux) will absorb six times their total weight in liquid. A 3-ounce roux will therefore absorb 18 fluid ounces of liquid to make 20 fluid ounces (2½ cups) of sauce.

The same 18 ounces can be thickened with 1 ounce of arrowroot. Arrowroot thickens without adding a taste of its own, it *clears* completely without "cornstarch cloudiness" and it thickens instantly at 212° F. The arrowroot is measured, placed in a bowl, mixed with a little water to form a thin cream-like consistency and then poured into a boiling liquid to thicken.

NUTRITIONAL ADVANTAGE:
Roux sauce base
1½ oz. butter plus 1½ oz. flour = 455 calories
Arrowroot sauce base
1 oz. arrowroot = 68 calories
20 oz. sauce makes approx. 6 servings; therefore
Roux base* is 74.5 calories per serving.
Arrowroot base* is 11.3 calories per serving.

SENSE ADVANTAGE. There is some downgrading of the finished sauce, especially if it is white. There is a texture loss, a feeling of "lack of substance," but the flavor is usually enhanced. Brown sauces do not suffer from these drawbacks nearly as much and they have the clarity plus factor.

* Note that this is for the base only, not the liquid or garnish used.

EFFORT ADVANTAGE. A considerable amount of time is saved.

BUDGET ADVANTAGE. Buy the arrowroot in 1-pound bags from good health-food stores, *not* in the small glass jars sold by herb-and-spice concerns.

For your next casserole (or stew), try adding *no* flour or thickening *at any stage.* Just before you serve it, skim off all the fat and strain off all the thin juices. Bring these to the boil and pour in the arrowroot, which has been mixed with a little water (about 1 tablespoon of arrowroot per cup of liquid to be thickened). Stir rapidly and return to the stew, fold in gently and serve. It will look brilliant and glossy, just like a *McCall's* food page!

Ⓜ *ARROWROOT can really help but needs a little understanding*

While arrowroot is very simple to use we have experienced some need for special care in the following areas:

- Don't purchase in small glass containers—it is prohibitively expensive packaged in that manner. Don't pay more than $1.50 per 2 pounds at a good reputable health-food store.*
- Liquid to be thickened *must* first be brought to the boil and then taken *off* the heat when the arrowroot "cream" is added; otherwise the cream can form hard dumplings by hitting the high heat source on the bottom. Return to heat and reboil to thicken.
- Stir the arrowroot "cream" just before you add it. The powder rapidly sinks to the bottom of the bowl.
- Add a little at a time; it is deceptive—you need very little to do the job and *too much* makes a dish look like a poorly set Jello! (One level tablespoon thickens 1 cup liquid to medium stage.)

NUTRITIONAL ADVANTAGE:

1 level tablespoon arrowroot = 48 calories
Replaces 2 tablespoons flour = 58 calories

BOILED CHICKEN

When next you boil a chicken, clear the fat from the surface and strain the cooking liquid through cheesecloth. Taste and add seasoning

* Price at time of writing.

if necessary. Measure out one cup, add 2 stalks celery (finely chopped) and boil for 5 minutes. Then add 1 tablespoon arrowroot mixed with 1 teaspoon soy sauce and 2 tablespoons table cream. Stir to thicken and pour over the jointed boiled chicken, dust with parsley and serve.

Ⓜ *MOZZARELLA is a "sauce" on its own*

The traditional shape of mozzarella is like a pear. The shape makes it easy to slice into rings and use as a *melted topping*. The idea is to use the cheese in lieu of a sauce. To do this all you have to do is cook your piece of fish, poultry, veal, beef, lamb or pork in a skillet, then drain off all the fat and cover the *cooked* food with the slice of cheese, sprinkle with a suitable "seasoning" such as sage for veal, tarragon for chicken, or capers for pork and *cover* the dish for 2 minutes. Then remove the "sauced" items and serve.

NUTRITIONAL ADVANTAGE:

	CALO-RIES	PRO-TEIN	CARBO-HYDRATES	TOTAL FAT	CAL-CIUM	VITAMIN A
Medium white sauce (4 oz.)	213	5.2 g.	12.1 g.	16.5 g.	148 mg.	655 I.U.
Mozzarella Cheese (2 oz.*)	168 (good)	16 g. (good)	.7 g.	11.1 g.	430 mg. (good)	NK

EFFORT ADVANTAGE. This saves the entire time it takes to make a sauce.

"SAUCED" CHICKEN

Cook breasts of chicken in a little oil in a skillet at a low heat. When cooked, pour off the fat, lay thin slices of mozzarella cheese on the surface and sprinkle with a few capers, anchovy fillets and parsley. Cover the dish and cook 2 minutes. Serve the coated chicken breasts dusted with paprika.

* Only 2 ounces of cheese is needed to replace the 4 ounces of sauce for 2 servings.

💲 *"INSTANT" MILK for cooking cuts cost and calories*

A large number of recipes call for *whole* milk. It's used in custards, sauces, puddings, and added to whipped potatoes, eggs, bread and soups.

However, non-fat milk in the *instant* form provides an interesting economy—when we take careful steps to reduce fresh consumption accordingly:

> 1 quart of milk made from "Instant" as per carton recipe costs 25¢.
> 1 quart of regular milk (which varies in price considerably) costs 37¢ to 45¢, a saving of 12¢ to 20¢ per quart.

For some dishes, however, the result is somewhat *thin* and, as a rule, we would suggest using an extra 1 ounce (3 tablespoons) to each quart of water which will change the cost to 33¢—giving a saving of 4¢ to 12¢ a quart, a *realistic* savings without taste loss. If you add a very little fresh grated nutmeg to "fill in the holes" left by the removal of the fat content, you can achieve a tastier product at realistic savings of about $18 per year without any suffering.

NUTRITIONAL ADVANTAGE. This is the profile comparison for various milks:

	CALORIES	PROTEIN	FAT	CALCIUM	RIBOFLAVIN
1 cup whole	160	9 g.	8.6 g. (3.5%)	288 mg.	420 mg.
1 cup "instant" per pkg. directions	90	9 g.	0.2 g.	298 mg.	440 mg.
1 cup "enriched instant" (see above)	113.8	12 g.	0.25 g.	390 mg.	453 mg.

BUDGET ADVANTAGE. For economy and also ease of doing this, we'd suggest buying bulk—not only are money savings greater, but it's also much easier to use the milk, since using 1 quart packages will necessitate opening another package when you want to add extra powder. For even greater ease and money saving we suggest that you buy in bulk and transfer the powder into airtight jars; don't store in the package—it can be messy, you may lose some and it will go stale if exposed to the air for a period of time.

💰 COCONUT "MILK" gets the flavor cracking in curry

A swift trip to the Polynesian or Indonesian Islands will give you ample justification to use coconut milk and cream. Both can be made from either the fresh, dried or frozen/canned pre-prepared creams or liquids.

Most of the fully prepared liquids have sugar added. For meat cookery, this is a real disaster area as the sweetening ruins the flavor of the dishes. So make your own, avoid a ruined dish and save some money!

The milk is made by placing 8 ounces of *grated*, not sweetened, white coconut flesh in a pan and covering it with 2½ cups vigorously boiling water—and allowing it to cool with a cover on it for 30 minutes. Then squeeze through muslin or cheesecloth. This produces 14 ounces of pressed coconut milk—quite enough to be used as a cooking liquid for, say, a neck of pork stew with green peppers and a light curry seasoning. The infused flesh can be infused once again but it will be so weak that it can only be recommended for cooking vegetables.

NUTRITIONAL ADVANTAGE. The food value profile is interesting. This is for 14 ounces, enough to provide flavor for a 4-portion casserole: 504 calories (bad); 6.4 g. protein (poor); 49.8 g. saturated fat (bad); 200 mg. phosphorous (good).

Obviously you need to be very sure that you are not on a fat free diet when you try this one.

KARE POAKA NO. 1
This is a dish that I had the honor of creating for Her Majesty the Queen Mother's visit to New Zealand in 1965.
(Serves 4)

2 lbs. pork (blade steak)   1 medium onion
Salt, preferably freshly ground   1 medium green pepper
Freshly ground black pepper   1 clove garlic

Juice of ½ lemon
1¾ cups (14 fl. oz.) coconut milk
(see above)
¼ cup ketchup
2 tbsp. sesame/safflower oil

1 tbsp. curry powder (mild)
1 tsp. mustard seeds
1 bay leaf
1 tbsp. red currant jelly
1 heaped tsp. chili powder

First prepare:

Make coconut milk. Remove fat from pork and cut into 2-inch cubes. Season with salt and pepper. Slice onion into 1-inch-wide rings. Cut pepper into 1-inch squares. Smash garlic. Squeeze lemon. Combine coconut milk with ketchup.

Now cook!

1. Heat oil in large saucepan, add meat and fry gently. Add onion and curry powder. Then add mustard seeds, green pepper, bay leaf and garlic and continue to fry gently stirring.

2. Pour in lemon juice, red currant jelly, ketchup and coconut milk. Simmer in open pot for 1½ hours. This is better made the day before.

3. Skim off all fat and pour off ¼ cup of the sauce. Blend this sauce with chili powder and pour into small sauceboat. This extra-hot sauce can be added by those who prefer "undemocratic curry."

STOCK *made as clear as a mountain stream*

Any stock that is used in a white or tomato sauce should simply be skimmed of fat and surface foam and then strained through a fine sieve.

A stock needed for a brown sauce thickened with arrowroot or one that is destined to become a consommé (clear soup) needs to be *clarified*—cleared of all "specks" of food. To do this you must first remove the fat, foam and obvious debris by straining. Add 1 beaten egg white for each 2 pints of stock to be cleared. Bring the stock to a slow boil. Take it off the fire and let the egg white settle. Bring to a slow boil again and remove. Skim off the egg with the "collected" particles firmly trapped within.

See "Carving in the Kitchen" (page 118) for an immediate use.

🕐 *STOCK made into ice cubes—a* ★★★★ *idea!*

The soup stock pot is an excellent example of European ingenuity when it comes to preventing waste. Essentially it's the place where all the trim goes. It can become a nondescript "broth." All dishes (except egg custard!!!!) benefit from good aromatic stock but the *makings* are not always at hand.

We make up a stock from a chicken carcass—or from some beef bones when we have them as a *natural by-product* from another meal. We clarify it and freeze it in ice cube trays—turning the cubes into a bag marked "Beef Stock" or "Chicken Stock," etc. Then all you need is one or two cubes and you are in business. You will find literally dozens of recipes in your own books and in mine that will help you to use this simple idea. Just keep the stock clearly of one type—chicken, or fish (see below) or beef or ham stock (see pages 119 and 163). For each pound of bones, add 1 cup (8 oz.) vegetable peelings and always add a bouquet garni (pages 161–62).

Remember—stock is always better than water!

See also "How to clarify stock" on page 171.

💲 *FISH STOCK makes a great soupmeal*

We once had the misfortune to consume a very poor fish soup in the south of France. Since that time I've wondered why such hugely varied results should occur from soup to soup. The answer, I am now convinced, lies in the head and the skin. We have conducted tests with straight "bones," with the head on its own, and again with head and skin.

The result of using only bones is clearly better, less muddy and more fragrant—so much better in fact that I strongly advise not using the head for fish soups or sauces.

FISH STOCK

Use 14 ounces bones (from 2½ to 3 pounds of whole fish), 1 medium onion, ¼ teaspoon thyme, 3-inch piece of celery, 1 bay leaf, 6 parsley stalks, 2½ cups water, ¼ teaspoon salt and ¼ teaspoon black pepper. Bring to the boil, reduce to barely moving simmer for 20 minutes, strain and use.

☺ *SEAFOOD SAUCE takes poached fish out of the "diet" bracket*

Poached fish, sauced, is somehow associated with ill health and diet times. In *fact* it is so good, from a taste point of view, that it is easily competitive with any other seafood technique. The problem lies in the liquid used to make the sauce and the thickening employed. It helps to make up a basic flour-and-butter roux first and to add to this milk to equal one-third of the liquid required. Three ounces of roux, made from 1½ ounces (6 tablespoons) of flour and 1½ ounces (3 tablespoons) of butter, can thicken 6 times its weight, or 18 ounces of liquid, so you would need to add 6 ounces (¾ cup) of milk to the roux and leave on a very low heat to *cook out* the uncooked roux taste.

For 4 servings, poach 4 5-ounce fillets of fish in 2 cups milk with a little onion, bay leaf, thyme, parsley, salt and pepper. When the fish is cooked, strain 1½ cups of the cooking liquor into the sauce and beat until smooth. Garnish according to recipe and coat the fish. In this way you avoid the delay caused in thickening the poaching liquid and you get a good "typical" sauce taste.

Of course, this "typical" taste is full, rich and quite high in calories. It is possible to replace the roux with arrowroot as shown on pages 166–67, but the richness is replaced by a thinner taste with less substance in texture.

NUTRITION COMMENT:
Typical Roux Style

1½ oz. flour (155 cal.) + 1½ oz. butter (300 cal.) + 6 oz. milk (113 cal.) = 568 cal.

Arrowroot Style

1 oz. arrowroot (68 cal.) + 6 oz. milk (113 cal.) = 181 cal.

A very small quantity (1 teaspoon) of soy sauce can be added to "make up" some of the richness lost by removing the butterfat.

SENSE ADVANTAGE in both cases makes an unremarkable inexpensive excellent protein food into a remarkable dish easily suited to a "company meal."

"A. J. ROCKFISH"

You will need four fillets of fish weighing about 7 ounces each. I like rockfish, striped bass or whiting—each poaches well and can look, as well as taste, excellent.

1. Lay the fillets in iced salt water (see page 98 for "crimping").

2. Prepare 2½ cups good fish stock (see pages 172–73).

3. Oil a skillet with 1 tablespoon oil, strain fish stock into it and bring to the boil, then reduce to simmer.

4. Take fillets straight from the iced water to the poaching liquid, cover and cook gently for 8 minutes.

5. During this time take 4 ounces of firm white mushrooms and slice them finely across the cap. Sprinkle with fresh lemon juice and cayenne pepper.

6. Remove fish when cooked with a long flat perforated "fish lifter" and keep them warm on their serving platter over a saucepan of boiling water.

7. Bring the cooking liquid to the boil and reduce it by rapid evaporation for 2 minutes. Dissolve 1 tablespoon of arrowroot in ¼ cup of milk and stir arrowroot into the hot (not boiling) cooking liquid. Return to heat and stir until it thickens.

8. Add enough table cream (about ¼ cup) to lighten the color and add 1 teaspoon of soy sauce (to replace the fat taken out by not using the roux-based sauce). Taste and adjust the seasoning.

9. Place mushroom pieces like large scales down the back of each fish fillet and coat with the hot sauce. Sprinkle with dillweed and a *little* cayenne pepper and serve.

Salads

(M) *MAYONNAISE that suddenly loses half* its calories*

Mayonnaise is one of those sauces that find general use in our day-to-day kitchens, over salads, in sandwiches, combined with tuna. We decided that it could be possible to create a light mayonnaise that would reduce calories and yet not limit taste, and that we could reduce the cost by increasing the volume.

By adding the beaten white of one egg we increased ½ cup mayonnaise to ⅝ cup, an increase of ⅛ cup. We added ¼ teaspoon of dillweed and a dash of cayenne to fill in the taste vacuum. It pours well, looks good, tastes excellent and has a fringe benefit. If you make your own mayonnaise and *curdle it*, you can repair the curdle by adding the whipped egg white slowly.

NUTRITION COMMENT. Mayonnaise has 100 calories per tablespoon; therefore ½ cup (8 tablespoons) has 800 calories. Since an egg white contains only 15 calories, you then get ⅝ cup for 815 calories and that reduces the new Light Mayonnaise to only 466 calories for ½ cup—and with the new seasoning we don't suffer.

BUDGET ADVANTAGE comes up by looking at the cost of an egg white—say 7¢—against the cost of ⅜ cup (6 tablespoons) mayonnaise, which is 21¢.† A pretty clear advantage even taking the dill and cayenne into consideration at less than a penny.

Simple recipes exist everywhere you have the need for regular

---

* Well . . . almost half!
† Prices at the time of writing.

mayonnaise. A tuna salad is especially good with this mixture—have fun!

🌹 FRENCH DRESSING "reformed"!

Most "French Dressings" served in the United States are tomato-mayonnaise style; in Europe "French Dressing" is *Vinaigrette*—rather similar to our "Italian Dressing."

In France the ratio of oil to vinegar is 2:1. I prefer the reverse, 1:2 —using a rice vinegar and adding a little sugar and mustard powder to compensate for the acidity.

NUTRITIONAL ADVANTAGE is high in both calorie reduction and fat reduction. Let's look at the comparative figures for 1 ounce of each:

	CALORIES	FAT	POLYUN-SATURATED FAT
European French dressing	192	21 g.	11 g.
"New" French dressing	86	9 g.	5 g.

As is clear from these figures, the "new" one is better for health—but what about the senses?

SENSE IMPACT comes from the acidity. The French, who consume wine with their day-to-day food, feel that a more acid dressing will "turn" their wine to vinegar. They may well be right, and you may wish to reverse the order *if you are serving wine;* otherwise I believe your body would appreciate a rest from so much oil.

WATERCRESS SALAD

Dip freshly rinsed and dried watercress in this recipe.

¼ cup sesame/safflower oil
½ cup rice vinegar
1 tsp. dry mustard powder
Freshly ground salt

Freshly ground black pepper
Sugar to taste (not more than 1 tbsp.)

Method:

Combine all ingredients and shake until sugar has dissolved. Always shake well immediately before using.

😊 AVOCADO as an aid to the dull salad

Avocado *in season* is a good buy, especially near or in the growing areas. You should look for "specials" at 3 for $1.00.* Select fruit that when held in cupped hands and pressed gently will "give" a little. (You can rapidly mature a hard avocado by placing it in a plastic bag with an apple and leaving it out of the refrigerator for a day.)

Cutting is best achieved by cutting into halves, then into quarters and then running a knife round *just under* the skin as you would remove the flesh from a melon slice. Once you've cut into an avocado, it is vital that you smother the cut slices with lemon juice the instant they are exposed to the air; otherwise the flesh discolors badly. As a matter of fact the lemon juice also helps the otherwise rather bland flavor of the fruit.

APPEARANCE ADVANTAGE is the greatest asset: there is a quality of luxury about a salad containing avocado slices. The gold and green coloring of the slices can add wonderfully to a mixed green salad.

NUTRITION ADVANTAGE lies mainly in its being a good source of Vitamin A—one-half of a good-sized fruit provides 290 I.U. (about one-third of the daily recommended allowance). There is a cautionary statement here. One half has 167 calories and such an expenditure places it quite high on the list of *avoidables* for anyone on a *strict diet*. So decide on a quarter of a fruit at 83.5 calories for salad use. Remember a little of even the "fattening" things brings you variety and variety is vital for your daily health.

AVOCADO SALAD
(Serves 4)

Cut the fruit into eighths and drench the slices in lemon juice. Make a dressing with 4 tablespoons sour cream, 1 tablespoon horse-

* Price at time of writing.

radish, salt and black pepper. Combine with the lemon juice which is strained, *at the last moment*, from the avocado slices. Lay 2 slices on a romaine lettuce leaf and coat with the sauce.

WESTERN ICEBERG LETTUCE, the c-c-crisp one!

When buying Western Iceberg Lettuce, note that the head should "give" slightly when squeezed. To make the best use of this green, strip off the outer leaves to use in sandwiches or in a cream of lettuce soup (see recipe below). Bang the core end of the lettuce hard onto the counter and twist out the heavy core. This avoids the use of a knife, which would discolor the cut surfaces.

Hold the head under the faucet with the cavity up and let a strong jet of cold running water flow into the lettuce. Turn it upside down and let it drain out thoroughly (this replaces some of the moisture lost in transit). When drained, put into a plastic bag, refrigerate and use as required.

NUTRITIONAL ADVANTAGE is found almost exclusively in its really low calorie value: 3½ ounces equals only 14 calories!

SENSE ADVANTAGE is textural: the crisp finish to this lettuce, when kept washed, drained and chilled like this, is *fabulous*. What it lacks in flavor it certainly makes up for in texture.

BUDGET ADVANTAGE is also good, especially when using a thick (1-inch) slice of lettuce as a "raft." Be careful to cut only at the last moment. Top the raft with slices of hard boiled egg and one slice of ham and coat with our Light Mayonnaise (page 175) and you've got a real plateful of emotion for next to nothing.

CREAM OF LETTUCE SOUP
(*Serves 4*)

1 lb. lettuce
1 large onion
2 tablespoons butter
¼ cup all-purpose flour
2 cups "cooking milk" (see page 169)

2 cups chicken stock
2 cloves garlic
Freshly ground salt
Freshly ground white pepper
Dillweed garnish

First prepare:

Thoroughly rinse lettuce and remove cores. Finely slice onion. Measure butter, flour, milk and stock. Smash garlic and chop to a pulp. Heat a soup tureen.

Now cook!

1. Place lettuce leaves in a large, dry saucepan and cook over medium heat for 6 minutes.

2. Place butter in another pan on low heat; stir in onion and let cook until soft. Stir in flour, making a roux. Cook 3 minutes, stirring.

3. Stir cooking milk into roux and add ½ of the chicken stock.

4. Remove cooked lettuce from pot, puree in a blender, return to pot and add soup. Add remaining chicken stock and cook while stirring for 7 minutes or until thickened. Season to taste with salt and pepper.

5. Strain lettuce soup through a sieve into soup tureen and serve at once with a dusting of dillweed.

Vegetables

(M) *KNIFEWORK for light vegetable chopping*

The right knife for chopping light vegetables and fruits such as onions, cucumbers, green peppers, tomatoes, green onions, green beans, asparagus, celery, zucchini, radishes, mushrooms, pineapples, avocados, apples, oranges, melons, pears, bananas, peaches, nectarines, etc. is the 8-inch French chef's knife. This blade is designed to be used in a specific manner by being guided by the curled-under first joints of the fingers. Thus the blade side must be completely smooth so that the blade can run up and down without cutting the fingers (hollow ground blades can not be used this way). I call this the "Fingernail Chop."

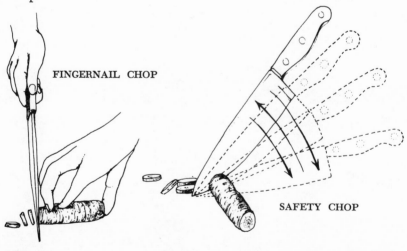

FINGERNAIL CHOP

SAFETY CHOP

180

You can move on to the tip-down *Safety Chop*. Here you must be able to *roll the blade* from tip to heel for best results while holding the tip to the board. This is an excellent way to finish a *fine chopping* procedure as for parsley and can be done with any blade that has a rounded edge.

NUTRITIONAL ADVANTAGE. The easy and correct use of French chef's knife will encourage use of fresh produce since many people stick to processed, dried or powdered products because they somehow "fear" the use of a sharp knife.

EQUIPMENT NOTE. I feel that a stainless steel blade has several advantages over straight carbon steel because it is less likely to rust and stain food *and* it will also hold its shape much longer. *Shape* is vital as you can see from the above techniques.

🪙 *LOW MOISTURE cooking is misunderstood*

It's a pity when our language gets the better of us and we say "waterless cooking" when we really mean "reduced water"! Perhaps "low moisture" is *less* likely to be misunderstood.

Although the low moisture concept is an excellent one many people see all vegetables as needing it. This isn't necessarily so. Such roots as carrot, parsnip and turnip for example contain only *small* amounts of water-soluble vitamins; their main claim to nutritional fame is in their Vitamin A content and this is not dissolved in water.

However, the interesting thing is that low moisture turns up trumps in the aromatic category and gives us a super treat at a low cost when we *partially fry* a mixture of root vegetables in a covered casserole at a low heat.

MIXED ROOT VEGETABLES

Cook a combination of carrots, parsnips, rutabagas and sweet potatoes in a very little clarified butter (see page 157) in a flameproof casserole covered with a tightly fitting lid. Toss well in the butter and season with salt and pepper. Cook slowly for approximately 25 minutes. Add *no* water or liquid—just let them cook in their own steam—then serve dusted with finely chopped fresh parsley.

CABBAGE AND ONIONS
(Serves 4)

8 oz. onions, in ¼" slices
24 oz. cabbage, in ¼" slices
1 tbsp. sesame/safflower oil
¼ tsp. salt

½ tsp. white pepper
1 tsp. dillweed
1 tbsp. parsley

Fry the sliced onions in the sesame/safflower oil until *just* softened but *not* colored.

Add the sliced cabbage, salt and pepper, toss together and cover tightly. Cook for 8 minutes over a medium heat, tossing from time to time.

When cooked but still crisp, add the dillweed and parsley, taste for other seasonings, turn into a dish and serve 4 huge portions at 100 calories per serving.

🕐 *CONTROVERSY will rage over this one!*

What is the best way to cook vegetables? Some think it is better to "blanch" green vegetables such as snap beans, broccoli, peas, broad beans and corn by boiling rapidly for a few minutes (number of minutes varies according to the vegetable) to establish the bright color. Then (saving the cooking liquor) the vegetables are turned into a little *iced* water to instantly stop the cooking. When cold, drain and cool-store ready for reheating. Just before service, the original cooking liquor is brought to the boil to simply reheat the vegetable. The question is—in the *average home* would this result in better-cooked vegetables than the normal "cook until tender" method? At present the vegetables compete with the main dish for last-moment attention and are frequently decidedly overcooked.

We would like to let you decide this one for yourself. There is a loss of Vitamin C in this new method, but since Vitamin C can be fairly easily found from our other daily foods, would we not be more excited by beautifully prepared vegetables?

BEANS IN GARLIC-FLAVORED BUTTER
(Serves 4)

1 lb. fresh green beans
1 clove garlic
2 tbsp. butter
½ cup cold water

Freshly ground salt
Freshly ground white pepper
Pinch of nutmeg

First prepare:

Trim and wash beans. Smash garlic. Measure butter. Put some ice in a bowl of cold water. Heat a vegetable dish in warming oven.

Now cook!

1. Place a small amount of water in a small saucepan and bring it to a boil.

2. Pop beans into boiling water and cook for 8 minutes.

3. Drain beans and immediately plunge them into iced water. Do not leave in the water once they are cool. This prevents their losing their beautiful color.

4. Return pan to heat, add garlic and butter and allow to sizzle.

5. Drain beans and toss them in garlic butter. Add salt and pepper and a pinch of nutmeg. Heat through and toss to cover the now glistening beans in garlic butter. Serve in heated vegetable dish.

BEAN AND BLACK OLIVE SALAD
(Serves 4)

1 lb. fresh green beans
Freshly ground salt
Parsley
Chives
1 medium onion
Freshly ground black pepper
Nutmeg
Black olives

French Dressing (¼ cup
    needed):
1 garlic clove
½ tsp. dry mustard
½ tsp. cayenne
1 to 2 tbsp. sugar
½ cup salad oil
1 cup rice vinegar
Yield: 1½ cups (12 fl. oz.)

First prepare:

Make French Dressing: Crush garlic and add with dry ingredients to oil. Add rice vinegar.

Wash and trim beans. Drop whole beans into salted boiling water and cook for 8 minutes. Drain. Finely chop parsley, chives and onion. Now assemble!

1. While beans are still warm, season with salt, pepper and nutmeg. Mix with onion.

2. Shake French Dressing well immediately before dressing salad so that oil and vinegar emulsify.

3. Toss beans with French Dressing and serve garnished with chopped parsley and chives and a few black olives.

($) *BEANSPROUTS can be grown at home—in time!*

Beansprouts are usually made from either mung beans, soy beans or alfalfa seeds. The technique is tedious to read about but easier to do! First measure ¼ cup of beans (quite adequate for a first effort). Now rinse them thoroughly in tepid water, drain and place in an opaque (not clear glass) bowl with a lid firmly on top. Each evening add more tepid water until the bowl is full, pour off and repeat. Scoop off any little green "husks" that float to the surface. Leave by the stoveside in the winter. Change the water twice each day and continue for 7 days until the beansprouts are at least 1 inch long overall. They are best to eat in salads at this length. The mung beans are best for cooking purposes and cost about 80¢ per pound compared with soy beans at 35¢ to 40¢. Ready-grown at the supermarket, sprouts usually cost 39¢ per pound.* As the mung grows to approximately 8 to 10 times its original weight, this means that by growing your own you wind up with 8 to 10 pounds of sprouts from 80¢ worth of beans—a saving of 29¢ to 31¢ per pound!

NUTRITIONAL ADVANTAGE includes low calories as well as contributions of iron and Vitamin C, as shown by this profile.†

	CALORIES	PROTEIN	CARBOHYDRATE	IRON	VITAMIN C
3½ oz. sprouted (raw)	35	3.8 g.	6.6%	1.3 mg.	19 mg.

* All prices at the time of writing.
† *Bowes and Church.*

BUDGET ADVANTAGE. Certainly cheaper (and better nutrition) to sprout your own rather than buy packaged sprouts.

BEANSPROUT SUGGESTIONS. One simple idea is to add 1 teaspoon sesame/safflower oil (page 159) to a large skillet. Throw in 2 cups of beansprouts, dash with 1 tablespoon of naturally brewed soy sauce, stir rapidly for *60 seconds*—just long enough to heat through—and serve to four people. A really delicious vegetable.

Another idea is to use them in your next salad—they add a really exotic touch at such a low cost.

MUSHROOMS *really work for everyone's menus*

This simple "vegetable" goes a long way to help our daily meals. It has a look of luxury yet when you see the quantity you get in one pound you have some idea of their advantage. They are also low in calories and take little effort or time to prepare and cook.

But, there are a couple of tricks (aren't there always!). If the mushrooms are cultivated, they won't need to be peeled, only washed. The washing should only be done *just before* they are cooked because a damp mushroom rots easily and gets discolored and slimy.

If you are frying them, simply place the mushroom tops in a lightly buttered pan, cap side down (gills up), and squeeze fresh lemon juice into the cap. Cook gently for 4 to 5 minutes, then turn over and cook briefly. Dust them with parsley and a *very little* cayenne and serve instantly.

Note: The stalks of cultivated mushrooms can be used in stock—don't just chuck them out!

SENSE ADVANTAGE. The well known greasy 'finish' of fried mushrooms is sidestepped—the lemon *stops* the fat from being absorbed by the gills. Therefore both taste and texture are helped.

NUTRITION COMMENT. Mushrooms are a great eating *reform* tool. 10 small mushrooms (or 4 large ones) raw have only 28 calories. If you add 1 teaspoon of butter for each *10*, then the total will be 61 calories and that's a gourmet's mouthful of flavor for the reformer who wants to lose weight and smile doing it!

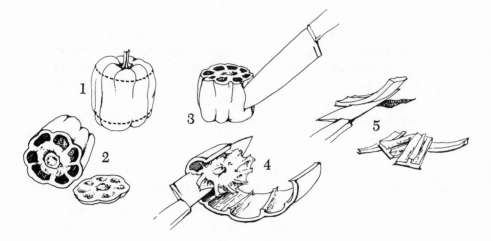

🌀 GREEN PEPPERS and that bothersome skin

The green or bell pepper—"Capsicum Annuum"—is accused by some authorities of being extremely indigestible; they insist that the skin should be removed by broiling to blacken the skin and subsequent scraping, or by deep frying for a moment or two and then the "scrape" job. Both are messy and time-consuming. I suggest that you cut the vegetable into quarters and, using a fine small sharp knife, cut just under the skin, pressing the skin to the board with the flat of the knife so that only the fine skin itself is removed. This is only necessary if you find you suffer discomfort, but please try them peeled just to compare.

NUTRITIONAL ADVANTAGE of the pepper lies in its being a super source of Vitamin C—providing it is not overcooked. Therefore, its use in salads in the raw state (with skin removed to prevent those cases of indigestion) preserves the maximum impact. Just look at this profile! One raw green pepper (3½ ounces): 22 calories (good); 420 I.U. Vitamin A (good); 128 mg. Vitamin C (very good!). When cooked: 18 calories (good); 420 I.U. Vitamin A (good); 96 mg. Vitamin C (still well over the recommended 45 mg. average daily allowance).

SENSES receive a real blessing from flavor, aroma, color and texture (especially when skinned).

BUDGET ADVANTAGE comes from better use when in season coupled with the use of the skin in soups/stocks. The skin must *not* be wasted, please!

CHILLED RATATOUILLE SALAD
(Serves 4)

⅓ cup sesame/safflower oil
1 small onion, sliced
2 cloves garlic, minced
2 medium green peppers, sliced
½ medium eggplant, sliced ¼-
    inch thick, unpeeled
2 medium zucchini, thinly sliced
    lengthwise
Salt and pepper
4 medium tomatoes, peeled and
    sliced
4 lettuce leaves

Dressing:
¼ cup sesame/safflower oil
½ cup rice vinegar
1 tsp. sugar
½ tsp. dry mustard
½ tsp. salt
½ tsp. ground black pepper
¼ tsp. cayenne pepper

First prepare dressing.

Heat oil in large skillet, add onion and cook until golden; add garlic, peppers, eggplant and zucchini. Fry vegetables gently. Season with salt and pepper. Cover pan tightly; simmer 30 minutes. Add tomatoes, allow to heat through. Transfer to bowl; chill. Serve cold on lettuce. Shake dressing well before adding to salad.

🌹 ONIONS, like people, can be different!

A swift visit to the average supermarket produce section will turn up an interesting array of onions. I'd just like to deal with three kinds:

Sweet Spanish cost me 89¢ for 1 pound.* Mild and sweet—the sweetness converts readily to a good color suited to soups like French Onion Soup where a mildness is also required.

Yellow Dried—"Downing Yellow Globe"—cost 23¢ per pound. These are pungent and have considerable holding power in sauces that need long cooking—they're especially good in curries where the onions have to "melt" with the spices to form a base.

* All prices at the time of writing.

Red Spanish—"Southport Red Globe"—cost $1.18 per pound and are a *salad* type onion suited to easy slicing. They should perhaps be "blanched" in boiling water 2 to 3 minutes for a salad for people with delicate digestions.

Since the Yellow Globe has the most flavor at the lowest cost, it follows that, for sound economic reasons, you should buy it for all stews and casseroles—in fact for our basic use.

NUTRITIONAL ADVANTAGE. One yellow globe onion (2¼ inches in diameter, raw) contains 38 calories. One-half cup cooked onion is listed at 29 calories.

Onions do also contain some B vitamins, a small amount of Vitamin C and the yellow-fleshed varieties also have some Vitamin A. However, these amounts would be considered insignificant.*

SENSE ADVANTAGE springs from taste and aroma. The onion is vital to successful cooking because *successful* cooking is aromatic and flavorful.

ONIONS WITHOUT TEARS

It is possible to avoid the annoying problem of crying while peeling onions by placing the onion into the deep freeze 15 minutes before use. This helps in reducing the spray of volatile oils that vaporizes

---

* *Bowes and Church.*

upon contact with a knife. You can also *skin* an onion easily: cut it into quarters and peel by slicing into the root end just under the outer skin and pulling back.

SENSE ADVANTAGE. The skins are useful in a good stock for both flavor and color (the brown skins produce an excellent amber color).

SIMPLE ONION SOUP

Take 1 pound of Bermuda onions, peeled and finely sliced to make 3½ cups. Shallow-fry in 1 tablespoon of sesame/safflower oil (see page 159) in a large heavy-based saucepan. Fry for 30 minutes in order to color but *not burn* the onions. Add 4 cups of good rich brown beef stock (see page 172). Bring to the boil, reduce heat to simmer and cook 30 minutes longer. Adjust the seasoning and serve. I do not add the usual bread and cheese for fairly obvious "reform" reasons. Just scatter the top with fresh parsley and enjoy!

BROCCOLI makes two vegetables in one

Some green leaf and "bud" vegetables have heavy stalks and light fragile leaves. If the *whole* plant is cooked until the stalk is tender then the leaves are frequently overcooked. A little ingenuity easily solves this problem. Using Broccoli as an example: Cut off the bud tops and slice the stalks in half lengthwise. Cook the latter in a little tomato juice, garlic and basil. This makes a "red" vegetable. The tops can be cooked later in very little water in a covered pot, making an excellent lightly steamed green vegetable from the same source.

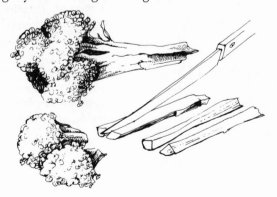

NUTRITIONAL ADVANTAGE comes from retained Vitamin C (lost when the tops are overcooked).

EFFORT ADVANTAGE is produced by getting two vegetables from the one source.

BUDGET ADVANTAGE results from the elimination of the excessive trimming that people do to the otherwise hard-to-cook stalks.

SENSES are jingled visually by the bright green of the buds and texturally by the crisp goodness of "both" vegetables.

TOMATOES *that show you care*

The outer skin of the tomato is ultra-thin but practically indestructible in normal cooking processes. When a tomato is chopped or sliced and then cooked, the skin toughens and remains long after its soft tissue has dissolved. These rolls or flakes of skin are unsightly and indicate a "lack of care." They can be removed easily by plunging tomatoes into boiling water for 60 seconds (or less) and then simply plunging them into cold or iced water. The skin just slips off without effort.

SENSE ADVANTAGE is the main benefit. I'm frankly of the opinion that "scruffy is as scruffy does" and that sloppy food preparation means a thoughtless cook. Those little rolls of tomato skin are a dead giveaway.

LITTLE PATTI TOMATOES

¼ tsp. dry mustard
½ tsp. cayenne
1 medium onion, finely diced
1 clove garlic, well crushed
1 tbsp. sugar (this is added to
   suit the dressing to local taste
   and is not classical)
½ cup olive oil
1 cup rice vinegar*

1 lb. medium tomatoes (8 per
   lb.), skins removed
Stalks of parsley, finely chopped
   (stalks only)
Leaves of lettuce heart, left
   whole for garnish
Very thin slices brown bread
   and butter, cut into quarters

* Good apple cider vinegar can also be used.

Note: The quantities for this sauce are more than adequate for the dish itself. This has been done on purpose in order to make available a surplus for the next you serve, but please be careful not to "soak" green salads in the mixture as the result is slimy, to say the least!

Method:

1. Mix mustard, cayenne, onion, garlic and sugar with olive oil. When sugar is dissolved, add vinegar; shake well.

2. Plunge tomatoes into boiling water, having first loosened the skin around the stem. Boil for 1 minute until you can see the skin begin to peel away from the stem area. But do not overcook, because the flesh becomes mushy.

3. Remove quickly and strip off the skin.

4. Place the peeled tomatoes in a small bowl, scatter top with chopped parsley and cover with the dressing; place in the refrigerator to keep overnight for best results.

5. Drain off the dressing. Slice tomatoes, lay them out on the lettuce, coat with a little dressing and serve very cold with the bread slices as a first course.

⑤ *SPINACH need not come in a bag*

It's good that at least one excellent green leaf vegetable should be enjoying volume sales. Spinach is one of the current Superstars and, as with all Superstars, part of the new image is the packaging.

Spinach is sold variously, but the keenest competition is between packaged in a plastic bag and loose and fresh. We conducted a test by buying *exactly* 1 pound of loose spinach for 59¢ and 10 ounces in a plastic bag for 55¢.* We kept both in the refrigerator for 2 days and then picked over, trimmed, washed and weighed the result. We found it took 2 minutes 26 seconds to pick over and trim the 16 ounces of loose leaves and that this produced 10 ounces, or 5.9¢ per ounce.

The bagged variety actually weighed 8 ounces when trimmed and took 2 minutes 12 seconds to prepare (only saving 14 seconds). It cost 6.87¢ per ounce. The saving per ounce was therefore 1¢, or 16¢ per pound.

If you use 2 pounds per week, the loose represents a saving of $16.64 per year—and it's *better* looking.

* Prices at the time of writing.

NUTRITIONAL ADVANTAGE. Spinach is 90.7 percent water. For each 3½ ounces you have this profile: 26 calories (good); 3.2 g. protein; 4.3 g. carbohydrate (good); 8,000 I.U. Vitamin A (good); 51 mg. Vitamin C (good). A thoroughly satisfactory vegetable which, I think, makes a great salad green.

SENSE ADVANTAGE. Spinach left as nature made it (not squashed in a plastice bag) looks better as a salad—it just seems fresher and larger and feels crisper.

SPINACH SALAD

Toss 10 ounces of washed, thoroughly dried and trimmed spinach leaves in French Dressing (page 176) and add 4 ounces finely sliced raw mushrooms with 1 tablespoon finely chopped green onions. You can add ¼ pound finely sliced, crisply fried and *drained* bacon pieces for a really super salad. Coat with the dressing at the last moment before service.

SQUASH suddenly becomes a French fry

French fried potatoes are one of the least satisfactory foods we have, from the nutritional aspect—yet they flourish because of the primal taste additive of salt and their color and aroma. *All* of this can be improved upon with fewer calories and less fat absorbed by using squash in lieu of potato.

SQUASH CHIPS

Cut Butternut Squash into "chips" 3 inches long by ½ inch thick. Cook in oil for 4 minutes at 320° F., drain and serve dusted with salt and chopped parsley.

Just in case you should decide that "this is for me," I give you below the actual saving involved—computed from an experiment conducted by the Department of Scientific and Industrial Research at my request in New Zealand.

NUTRITIONAL ADVANTAGE. French fried potatoes were cooked for 5 minutes at 300° F. in oil and then for 6 minutes at 375° F. French-fried squash were cooked for 4 minutes at 320° F.

The French-fried potatoes contain approximately 272 calories per 100 grams (3½ ounces). The squash chips contain approximately 190 calories per 100 grams. The squash chips thus provide fewer calories per unit weight. This is quite obviously not an overnight Dietrich Diet —as diets go this should still be a "watch-it" food—but if the "French fry urge" overwhelms you, then go squash—not potato!

SENSE ADVANTAGE lies in a pretty broad coverage. The squash fries *look* better, *taste* better, *smell* better and have a better *texture*.

EFFORT PROBLEM comes up due to the extreme toughness of the squash. You need a large French-chef's knife to handle it. On the other hand there is a saving in cooking time.

VEGETABLE DISHES in one dish for a complete meal

The idea behind this section-within-a-section is to give you a concept "proposal": that we try to produce one complete meal from vegetables every so often.

It has been suggested by some Government officials that one "no meat" meal could provide valuable grain foods for developing countries, but this suggestion didn't come complete with a series of attractive all-in-one-dish recipes. This is why we have included them and why I believe you should give them a go. I also include the nutrition profile with each dish.

VEGETABLE DISH NO. 1
CABBAGE
(*Serves 4*)

Incredibly quick with few ingredients—these are the classic advantages of this vegetable "Super Dish."
For 4 servings:

1 tbsp. butter
1½ lbs. white cabbage, sliced
   into ¼ inch strips

3 stalks celery, finely sliced
2 medium carrots, grated
1 tsp. dill weed, dried

1 tbsp. chopped parsley
2 tsp. fresh chopped mint (if not
   available then leave the recipe
   until it is)
Salt and white pepper to season

2 large tomatoes, cut in halves
   and broiled lightly
6 oz. Dutch Gouda or Edam or
   U.S. Cheddar (preference
   order), cut into ½-inch cubes—
   no larger

Melt butter in a large deep pan over medium heat. Add cabbage, season and toss well (lid on!). Cook 4 minutes only. Add celery, carrot, herbs, salt and pepper. Toss well, cover and cook 4 minutes. Cut lightly broiled tomatoes in cubes and add with the cubed cheese, stir carefully and serve immediately.

NUTRITIONAL PROFILE (per serving)

	CALORIES	PROTEIN	CARBOHYDRATE	TOTAL FAT	POLY-UNSATURATED FAT	VITAMIN C	VITAMIN A	CALCIUM
with Edam	241	15.6 g.	19 g.	11.9 g.	.3 g.	205 mg.	6,430 I.U.	341 mg.
with Cheddar	279	14.7 g.	18.2 g.	16.8 g.	.5 g.	205 mg.	6,218 I.U.	318 mg.

A low-calorie meal, good source of protein, Vitamins A and C.

VEGETABLE DISH NO. 2
VEGETABLE PILAF
(Serves 4)

Another Vegetable Dinner fully prepared in one dish.

2 tbsp. safflower oil
2 carrots, diced
2 medium onions, diced
1 cup long grain rice
1 stalk celery
1 bay leaf
¼ tsp. powdered thyme
2½ cups Ham Hock Stock (page
   163)
¼ lb. small mushrooms

2 oz. snap beans
¼ lb. lima beans
3 tbsp. raisins
2 tbsp. split almonds
¼ lb. peas
1 large tomato
Salt
½ tsp. basil
(Tabasco and soy sauce on the
   side)

Heat oil in an ovenproof casserole (4-quart size). Shallow-fry carrots, onions, rice and celery, in the order given, over a medium heat, stirring often, for approximately 10 minutes. Add bay leaf, thyme, and stock, cover and place in 425° F. oven for 25 minutes. After 10 minutes add mushrooms and snap beans, stir in. After 5 more minutes add lima beans, raisins, almonds and peas, stir in. Slice tomato into thin rings, salt and dust with basil. Cover the vegetables with the tomato as a topping and serve immediately.

NUTRITIONAL PROFILE (per serving)

CALORIES	PROTEIN	CARBO-HYDRATE	FAT	POLYSATU-RATED FAT	VITAMIN C	VITAMIN A
443	12 g.	73 g.	12 g.	6 g.	34 mg.	5,000 I.U.

This one-dish meal is relatively low calorie, and a *good* source of Vitamin A. Protein is of good quality since you're combining 2 "incompletes" (legume-type and rice) which complement each other to produce a "complete."

VEGETABLE DISH NO. 3
PLATED CABBAGE
(*Serves 4*)

Boil 4 4 oz. potatoes in their skins for 20 minutes and dry out in a covered warm dry saucepan (see page 199 for technique).

Strip off a dozen dark green outer leaves from 1 cabbage and cut out the heavy white center veins. Boil the leaves rapidly for 2 minutes until bright green; strain and cool in a bowl of iced water.

Peel and slice finely 2 medium onions, and fry in a large deep pan in 1 tablespoon of vegetable oil (safflower for preference). Add 1 pound finely sliced cabbage (¼-inch thick strips). Cover and cook over medium heat for 4 minutes, then add 1 tablespoon soy sauce, 1 tablespoon chopped parsley, ½ teaspoon dillweed and 1 teaspoon white pepper. Stir together thoroughly and cover for 2 minutes.

Grease (or oil) a large tart or pie dish and cover with the 6 best green cabbage leaves. Slice the potatoes and lay them over the entire surface. Season with salt and pepper and coat with 2 tablespoons melted butter.

Then slice 1 medium tomato into very thin slices. Make a layer of these over the potatoes; season with salt and pepper.

Now heap on top the chopped seasoned cabbage, cover with the remaining green leaves and press down tightly with another plate. Reheat by placing the dish *over* a boiling saucepan. Serve on the plate cut up into four like a green pie!

P.S. Sliced and fried bacon can be added for extra flavor.

NUTRITIONAL PROFILE (per serving)

CALORIES	PROTEIN	CARBOHYDRATE	TOTAL FAT	POLYUNSATURATED FAT	VITAMIN C	VITAMIN A
192	6.2 g.	36 g.	3.8 g.	2.6 g.	120 mg.	694 I.U.

This dish is high in Vitamin C from *cabbage,* potato and tomato; it also has significant Vitamin A from *tomato,* cabbage. Cooking the potatoes in their skins and the cabbage for only a short time preserves maximum Vitamin C.

VEGETABLE DISH NO. 4
CASSEROLE IN CREAM SAUCE
(Serves 4)

This is an excellent 25-minute vegetable casserole that takes only about 10 minutes' preparation time. It's a one-dish effort and tastes *super.*

1 tbsp. safflower oil
2 medium carrots, diced
8 small onions
¼ lb. snap beans
1½ cups sliced green onion
¼ lb. cauliflower "tops"
  (flowerettes)
¼ lb. small mushrooms
1 cup Ham Hock Stock*

2 tbsp. arrowroot or fecule,†
  mixed to a thin paste with a
  little milk
1 cup milk
1 heaped tbsp. chopped parsley
1 cup frozen peas, thawed
1 cup frozen lima beans, thawed
¼ cup grated cheese

* Make stock from a 1-pound ham hock (see page 163) and trimmings from first 6 vegetables—see page 121 for technique.
† Fecule—refined potato starch—is also called Kartopfel Meal; imported by Holly Woods, Inc., Colorado Springs, Colorado 80901.

Pour oil into a large skillet. Add carrots, onions, snap beans, green onion, cauliflower and mushrooms *in order given* and fry over medium heat with lid on. Do not season. Add stock, cover and cook at a barely moving simmer for 10 minutes. Add arrowroot paste, boil, and add milk. Stir in parsley, peas and lima beans. Turn into a flameproof casserole, dust with cheese and broil for 5 minutes, until just browned. Serve very hot, preferably on brown earthenware plates.

NUTRITIONAL PROFILE (per serving)
With stock

CALO-RIES	PROTEIN	CARBOHY-DRATE	TOTAL FAT	POLYUN-SATU-RATED FAT	VITAMIN C	VITAMIN A
296	11 g.	38.7 g.	12.3 g.	5.3 g.	54 mg.	9,906 I.U.

This casserole is high in Vitamin A (carrots) and Vitamin C (cauliflower and other vegetables); it has some high-quality protein as well as calcium from milk and cheese. Stock made with ham hocks supplies small quantities of thiamine, as ham is high in this B vitamin. There are small amounts of iron from vegetables, particularly lima beans and peas, but overall iron content is not high.

Starch

🌹 *BREAKFAST fondue is a whole lot of fun for everyone!*

Breakfast cereals are subject to all kinds of whims and fancies and can result in the table center's looking like a cardboard Manhattan. But a new way can be found for a warming cool-weather breakfast that everyone can discover as his own. Breakfast Fondue!

Depending on your diet (or "reform") situation and *climate* you can make the basic "Cream of Wheat" with either instant milk (less expensive and fewer calories plus less fat) or with whole milk. I favor the latter because the taste is dramatically different, and to start the day well seems important to me!

For 4 people, use 1 scant cup (6 ounces) cream of wheat to 3½ cups milk and cook as per package with *no* sugar. This is served in that Fondue Pot that you purchased but only used once! or doled out into bowls as normally. The treat comes from the small bowls (better if they match) placed on a Lazy Susan filled with such things as granola, wheat germ, raisins, sliced dried apricots, chopped nuts, honey, All Bran or fresh fruit. The list is endless and it's great fun to create your very own breakfast just as you feel like it—*every day!*

NUTRITIONAL ADVANTAGE is rather obvious because it provides for a wide variety of flavors and textures to be added to an excellent basic cereal.

SENSE ADVANTAGE is complete: we have texture, color, flavor, aroma and taste all wrapped up in a fun idea. Is there anything else you can add?

198

EFFORT ADVANTAGE comes from the reduction of all that fussing about with eggs, bacon, etc., etc. The cream of wheat can be made the night before and left in a double boiler top in the refrigerator. In the morning you need only stagger to the stove, plop the "top" in the "bottom" of the double boiler and safely reheat it *without looking* as you ready the toast, juice and put out the bowls of "goodies." It really is simple stuff.

⊛ POTATOES *boiled with a towel!*

A potato should not be waterlogged! Many times the poor old boiled potato is left to soak up its cooking liquids like a sponge. A good way to avoid this is to select potatoes that are *all* of medium to small size (about 2 inches long). Scrub them well, leaving the skins intact. Place in warm salted water, cover and bring to the boil. Cook for 15 minutes—test with long needle or fine skewer (the potato should *just* slide off). Pour off the water, reduce heat to very low, set the pan back on the heat and cover the potatoes tightly with a clean dry terry towel and the lid of the pan. Leave for 5 minutes and the potatoes will steam themselves "dry." Be sure to tuck the towel in!

NUTRITIONAL ADVANTAGE. One hundred grams (3½ ounces) of potato has the same Vitamin C content whether pared before or after boiling: 16 milligrams.* There is a slightly higher value of minerals and B vitamins in the unpared potato. Calories: 76 per 100 grams (2½-inch diameter potato).

BUTTERED AND HERBED NEW POTATOES
(*Serves 4*)

2 lb. tiny new potatoes	Pinch of salt
1 bunch parsley	4 tbsp. butter
1 bunch mint	

First prepare:
Rinse potatoes. Do not remove skins. Put a pot of water on to boil. Wash parsley and mint and chop the leaves, but leave the stalk whole.

---

* *Bowes and Church.*

Heat a vegetable dish in warming oven.

Now cook!

1. Pop potatoes into boiling water with a pinch of salt. Add parsley and mint stalk. Cover with a tightly fitting lid.

2. Boil for 20 minutes on high heat.

3. Drain cooked potatoes and submerge in cold, running water. Rub them between your hands and skin will come away more easily than by any other peeling method.

4. Return potatoes to a pan with melted butter and cover with a clean cloth. Place over lowest heat (if gas please use a heat pad to avoid direct contact).

5. Remove cloth and dust potatoes with chopped mint and parsley leaves. Place in the vegetable dish and serve.

POTATO, friend or foe?

Fad dietmongers frequently fall upon the potato as a starch/carbohydrate/calorie-filled no-no! In truth it only becomes a villain through additives, not the wonderful tuber itself!

Look at this potato (which, incidentally, weighs 100 grams or 3½ ounces).

- Raw, it has only 76 calories, the same as parsnip and sweet corn, and it contains 20 mg. of Vitamin C, about one-third the daily recommended allowance of 55–60 milligrams.
- Baked in its jacket, 90 calories (due to moisture loss) and the same 20 mg. Vitamin C.
- Baked in its jacket, with 2 tablespoons butter added, 290 calories and 20 mg. Vitamin C.
- Baked in its jacket, plus 3 tablespoons sour cream/chives, 165 calories and 20 mg. Vitamin C.
- Boiled in its skin and then skin removed, 77 calories, which is same as before for raw (*but more if steam dried*, see page 199) and 16 mg. Vitamin C.
- Skinned and then boiled, 65 calories and 16 mg.* Vitamin C.
- Boiled, skinned and buttered (2 tablespoons per serving), 277 calories and 16 mg. Vitamin C.

* Only 4 mg. are lost when skinned—this proves that the major Vitamin C content is *not* in the skin.

- Mashed with milk added, a ½-cup serving has 63 calories; plus 1 teaspoon of butter, 94 calories—and 9 mg. Vitamin C.
- French fries (100 g. or 20 pieces), 310 calories and 21 mg. Vitamin C.

NUTRITION COMMENT. To help you with your estimate of the effect of the additive, let's just give you a list of the enemies.

• 1 tsp. butter (1 pat)	35 calories
• 1 tbsp. butter	100 calories
• ¼ cup milk for mashed potatoes	40 calories (about 10 calories per serving)
• 2 tbsp. sour cream	50 calories
• 1 tsp. blue cheese	18 calories
• 2 tbsp. skim milk, yoghurt	16 calories
• ¼ tsp. dillweed	1–?

The recipe idea after all this information is really up to you!

POTATO BAKED in its jacket is a prince of the plate providing . . .

That it isn't drenched in butter or sour cream! Also the practice of baking a potato in a jacket of foil has been made popular by the "pincer" movement attack on the left flank by the Restaurants and on the right from the Barbecue. In neither case does it make sense that our own home ovens should follow suit.

BAKED POTATO

Scrub the potato, preferably a Burbank Russet from Idaho (large and long—about 10 to 12 ounces each), which can be cut in half for good size portions. While the potato is still wet, roll it in a *little* salt. Trim a penny-sized piece from one end to allow steam to escape and bake on the oven rack at 375° F. for 1 hour 15 minutes. Before cutting open, wrap a towel about the potato and squeeze it carefully to break up the inside flesh; then cut and dust with ½ ounce grated parmesan cheese, brown under the broiler and serve dusted with parsley.

SENSE ADVANTAGE is in a wonderfully crisp exterior (which is usually steamed soggy by its foil coating) and a light floury fragrant interior topped and crusted with cheese.

NUTRITION COMMENT. A half potato (about 3½ ounces) served this way has 90 calories and 20 mg. of Vitamin C. So it is by no means an enemy to the "reformer." Remember it's what goes *on* that is harder to take *off*, and the 30 calories of cheese (1 tablespoon) can replace the 100 or so represented by the butter or polyunsaturated spreads.

SPECIAL BAKED POTATOES

Purchase a jar of pickled walnuts from a gourmet shop. Now fry about 4 slices of bacon which are cut into 1 inch sections until crisp. Open the baked potato and spoon out all the flesh. Beat smooth with a *little* milk, season with salt and white pepper, add 1 tablespoonful of chopped pickled walnuts and 1 teaspoon of chopped cooked bacon pieces, together with some fresh chopped parsley. It looks and tastes *wonderful*. You can use bacon alone but the walnuts add a *special* touch.

RICE can be fluffy and separate

A major goal in *most* nations' rice cookery is to achieve separate, fluffy, independent or *solo* grains. Clogged starchy rice masses are not, as a rule, enjoyed. Clog happens through overcooking in too great a volume of water and from surface starch created by movement of the rice against itself in packing and shipment. The obvious first step must be to rid the rice of its surface starch by rinsing under cold water until the water runs clear. *CAUTION:* Don't rinse the rice marked as "enriched" or having "added nutrients," as these are put into the package in powder form. My recommendation would be to avoid these "nutrients added" products *unless you consume a great deal of rice in lieu of bread.*

For the *solo* effect you will need long-grain converted rice which is well washed and scattered into 1 quart boiling salted water for each cup of rice. Boil for 10 minutes only and turn into a metal colander or steamer (with small holes). Then return to the original pan and place a smaller lid inside to cover the rice *in* the colander. Add ¼ cup water to the bottom of the pan to prevent burning. Then steam for a further 5 minutes.

Each grain will be "solo" and fluffy. This will *always* work, if you follow these directions exactly.

SENSE ADVANTAGE is substantial visually, with textural backup.

EFFORT ADVANTAGE is due to the extreme simplicity of the idea.

BUDGET ADVANTAGE. An ordinary long-grain converted rice costs about 41¢ per pound as against a Minute Rice product with added nutrients at 65¢ per pound.* Yearly savings could amount (for 2 rice meals per week for a family of four) to $9.24, saving 24¢ per pound.

SHELLY BAY RICE
(*Serves 4*)

*½ cup sultanas, soaked in water
   before measuring
½ cup bamboo shoots; or the
   center core of a fresh pine-*
*apple; or the center core of a
cabbage; or the white of chard
—in all cases finely diced to the
size of a pea*

* Prices at the time of writing.

2 tbsp. soy sauce
1 medium carrot, finely diced
1½ stalks celery, finely diced
½ small onion, finely diced

1 cup long-grain rice, well
    washed
1 tsp. salt
Garnish: a few very green raw
    peas

Method:

1. Soak the sultanas and finely diced vegetables in the soy sauce for at least 15 minutes before cooking.

2. Wash the rice very thoroughly. Salt 3 pints of water, bring to the boil and add the rice. Stir and leave simmering for 10 minutes.

3. Drain the rice in a colander—but please do *not* run it under either the cold or hot tap.

4. Place the colander on top of a saucepan of 1 to 1½ cups of boiling water and add the vegetables, sultanas and soy sauce to the rice, mixing them in well.

5. Place the saucepan lid on top of the rice and steam in this way for 5 minutes. The water level in the saucepan should not reach the bottom of the colander when it boils.

6. Turn the now perfect rice out into a warmed serving dish and serve immediately, garnished with the raw green peas.

$ RICE that soaks up the flavor as it cooks

Plain boiled or steamed rice does have the problem of being rather bland and certainly non-aromatic. One way in which this grain can be "enhanced" is to make a Pilaf, so that it absorbs flavor and aroma as it cooks.

PILAF
(Serves 4)

Finely chop 1 small onion. Shallow fry gently in 1½ tablespoons sesame/safflower oil (page 159). Stir in 8 oz. rice (long grain) and fry for 3 minutes. Add these herbs tied in a square of cheesecloth: 1 sprig thyme, 6 parsley stalks, 1 3″ stalk of celery and 1 bay leaf. Add 2½ cups stock (the flavor suited to the dish, i.e. fish stock with fish or shellfish, chicken stock with poultry dishes, etc.). Season with salt and pepper and bake *uncovered* for 20 minutes at 450° F. Remove herbs and serve.

BUDGET ADVANTAGE. This is a wonderful dish for budget stretching without suffering. Literally any small amount of cooked meat, grain or bean protein or bright green vegetable such as spinach can be added when the rice leaves the oven. Just stir it in and serve with a crisp side salad, it's super!

NUTRITIONAL ADVANTAGE. The food profile is for 1 serving (25 percent of the recipe given): 315 calories (good); 55 g. protein; 56 g. carbohydrate; 4 g. total fat (good).

(◔◡◔) *NOODLES can be variety in themselves*

Egg noodles are a fine variety starch food for our day-to-day meals. Unfortunately they often get used in the typical "Restaurant" way. By this I mean recipes that are set up to seem "special" and satisfy "cash customers." You do this by adding eggs, cream, butter, bacon, cheese, sauces. By all that is fattening, isn't it enough to simply serve a noodle plain!

Well, obviously not! So here we have a very simple idea that uses a basic consommé. Just cook the noodles in a rich stock or meat broth, reduce the cooking liquid, thicken with a *little* arrowroot (16 calories per teaspoon) and add fresh herbs. Variety without insult, Praise the Lord!

NUTRITIONAL BENEFIT is the absence of heavy fat concentrations typical in the serving of this kind of food.

SENSE ADVANTAGE is found mainly in the visual and aromatic area.

NOODLES IN STOCK

Add 1 tablespoon soy sauce to 1 cup of good dark meat stock (see Stock Cubes, page 172). Bring to the boil and add 2 ounces dried noodles (preferably the bundled Chinese egg noodles) per person. Increase stock if you are cooking for more than 4. Cook according to the packet directions until "al dente"—just firm to the bite. Then turn out, retain the stock, bring it to the boil; mix 1 teaspoon arrowroot and 1 tablespoon fresh chopped parsley with a little cold water to a cream-like consistency and pour this into the boiling stock. Stir briskly, adjust the seasoning to taste and pour over the noodles. Serve immediately.

☺ SPAGHETTI that lets go!

The best cooked spaghetti is firm to the teeth ("al dente") and doesn't stick to itself! To achieve this we cook the spaghetti in vigorously boiling salted water for about 8 minutes (varies according to the manufacturer). When cooked, for every 8 ounces spaghetti add 1 pint of *ice* cold water to the pan, stir twice and turn the pasta out into a colander ready for use. When it is drained, toss it in a little oil or butter or a mixture of the two, seasoned, sauced or garnished according to the recipe, and serve *instantly*—it should never sit and steam itself flaccid!

NUTRITIONAL ADVANTAGE comes from the degree of cooking. Here we have a gain in the nutritive "merry-go-round" and a loss on the calorie "swings."

The proposed technique would eliminate the overcooking problem and excess loss of water-soluble nutrients. I do not have precise data on the nutritive value of the product cooked according to this suggested method. However, food value tables do distinguish between macaroni cooked to firm stage and cooked until tender:

Macaroni (enriched) 1 CUP	CALORIES	PROTEIN	CARBOHYDRATE	THIAMINE	RIBOFLAVIN	NIACIN
cooked, firm	190	6 g.	39 g.	.23 mg.	.14 mg.	1.8 mg.
cooked, tender	155	5 g.	32 g.	.20 mg.	.11 mg.	1.5 mg.

SPAGHETTI CARBONARA

5 oz. ham hock "bacon meat"
  (or bacon slices*)
Salt
2 oz. Parmesan cheese (solid
  piece)

3 eggs
Black pepper
10 oz. spaghetti
1 tbsp. safflower oil
1 tbsp. fresh chopped parsley

First prepare:

Finely dice bacon into ¼-inch cubes. Place pot of salted water on high heat. Have 2½ cups of ice water ready in refrigerator. Finely grate the Parmesan cheese; beat the whole eggs in a bowl with a fork and season with black pepper and a *little* salt.

Now cook!

1. "Curl" spaghetti into boiling salted water and cook for approximately 8 minutes until *just* tender ("al dente").

2. Take pan from the heat and add the iced water. Stir and pour into a colander. *Do not rinse.*

3. In a large saucepan fry the finely cubed meat in the oil until lightly crisped.

4. Add the drained spaghetti and toss until completely coated in the oil and bacon fat.

5. Pour in the beaten eggs and fold over and over in order to cook the eggs completely.

6. You can add half the cheese and toss again or serve the cheese separately if some members of your family prefer the taste of uncooked cheese.

7. Turn onto a dark platter or into a pottery casserole dish. Dust with parsley and serve immediately.

* Hock bacon can reduce the cost.

Desserts

🌹 *FRUIT with bruise can amuse!*

This one will really depend upon the fruit concerned but, in general, those fruits that have stones—nectarines, peaches, plums—can become badly bruised and tend to be thrown out. There is another way and it's delicious!

FRUIT COMPOTE

Cut away all bruised parts of fruit and add 1 ounce (2 table-spoons) water to each ounce of fresh fruit. (1 pound fruit = 2 cups water) To each cup of water add ½ ounce (4 teaspoons, packed) brown sugar and 1 tablespoon fresh lemon juice plus a small piece (1 by 2 inches) of lemon peel.

Bring to boil slowly for 10 minutes, remove fruit pieces to bowl and reduce liquid to only ¼ cup of syrup. Stir syrup into the fruit and cool.

NUTRITIONAL ADVANTAGE comes exclusively from the fruit and therefore is big on Vitamin A. Whichever fruit you use, the one common factor is the syrup. This has a profile for 4 servings of: 56 calories, 14.6 g. carbohydrate, 3 I.U. Vitamin A.

Add this to the plain fruits, which have these profiles:

	CALORIES	CARBOHYDRATE	VITAMIN A	
½ lb. peaches	87	22.2 gm.	1,810 I.U.	
½ lb. nectarines	183	49.0 gm.	4,725 I.U.	
½ lb. plums	189	51.0 gm.	860 I.U.	(Damson)
			or 3,840 I.U.	(Italian or Imperial)

and that looks like really good news to me!

SENSE ADVANTAGE. Splendid taste and appearance.

BUDGET ADVANTAGE. Bruised fruit should cost you half the cost of the original* and wind up, in volume, saving you 25 percent (after cutting away bruised parts). When compared with prepared foods, the sky gets to be the limit for your savings.

For a "sweet 'n sour" dessert, try a spoonful over ice cream.

As a fruit base for homemade yoghurt (see page 212), its delicious.

For a spiced "dressing" for roast "young" meats—pork, veal, lamb, poultry—add ¼ teaspoon allspice.

☺ *CANDIED ORANGE AND LEMON ZESTS are a non-moreish nibble*

If you have a sweet tooth yet would like to be creative, then the use of both orange and lemon peel as a sugared candy might provide an unusually low cost/high interest piece of individualism.

CANDIED ORANGE AND LEMON ZESTS

Cut the skin from 2 oranges and 2 lemons in quarters. Place these in cold water to cover, bring to boil and throw out the water. Cover with cold water once more and simmer; this for 20 minutes. Remove from heat, cool and peel off any surplus white flesh (in heavy-skinned fruit only). Dissolve 2 cups of sugar in 1 cup water. Slice the skins into ¼-inch thick strips, place in the syrup and simmer for 30 minutes. Lift

---

* I am advised that in such major cities as New York bruised fruit is never made available at a discount, which, I guess, is another good reason for living elsewhere!?

pieces with a slotted spoon onto a large plate covered with 1 cup sugar. Toss to coat with sugar and lay them out on waxed paper to dry. Place in *airtight* decorative bottle until needed.

SENSE ADVANTAGE is with the initial sweet taste followed up by an exceptionally powerful wallop from the super flavor oils left in the skins. The texture is hard yet chewy and they last and last.

NUTRITION COMMENT. I cannot eat more than one piece at a time. The flavor is such a "knockout" that it completely satisfies me for hours. You know most candies are designed to leave you feeling like having another one the instant you've finished it. So if you *absolutely crave a mouthful of flavor* then here it is and the flavor will last!

☺ SUGAR CUBES *full of natural flavor*

The flavors of lemon and orange zest (the fine outside skin) are unique in the modern kitchen. The residual flavors are extraordinary and, when stored in sugar cubes, remain fresh and available without presenting texture problems as the grated or sliced peels do. Best of all—they're FREE!

Next time you peel an orange or a lemon, take the peel and lay it out flat (can be peeled in quarters for easier handling). Then rub the outer skin hard with each of the six sides of a cube of sugar. Store in a tightly covered jar until you want a *real* orange or lemon flavor in your cakes, cookies or, better still, your custards—and they are especially good in fruit sauces for crepes (see next page).

SENSE ADVANTAGE comes from flavor, aroma and texture. It is just wonderful how these sugar cubes are saturated with the sharp natural flavor of the fruit. Somehow the reward is at least the equal of the effort.

NUTRITION COMMENT is needed here to explain that, while refined sugar is a *diet* no-no, it doesn't mean that it must *never* be consumed. Some folk rush off to buy raw sugars and honey as substitutes and convince themselves that because it is slightly (and I mean slightly) better, that "better" means "good for you." There is no validity in that feeling. I believe that if you must have sugar in a dessert, let it be the best sugar for the job—and that sugar is almost always refined! So here we use a technique that uses its unique ability to pick up natural flavor oils. *Just one point!* Try to use less sugar than that specified in *every* recipe, including mine. Train your tooth *down* to a level, not up! Many cake and cookie recipes can be cut by ⅓ to ½ of their sugar content and actually taste better.

(◕‿◕) *PANCAKES that make a delicious dent in the diet*

We have discovered an attractive dessert for you. Relatively low in calorie and fats, high in appearance appeal, low in cost and deliciously sweet and sour.

THIN PANCAKES (CREPES)

Combine 1 whole egg (medium size), 1 egg yolk, 1⅛ cups (9 fl. oz.) milk and 1 cup flour. Mix all ingredients completely and let stand 4 hours. Make pancakes as shown on pages 88–89 and here is the sauce: Crush 4 cubes sugar (can be 2 orange, 2 lemon "zested" cubes—see preceding page) in 2 tablespoons butter, cook to light fudge (slightly browned), add 1 cup freshly squeezed orange juice and stir to combine. Add 8 crepes to the sauce one at a time, folding in half then in half again until all 8 are added. Then add ½ cup plain natural yoghurt to the orange sauce, stir and serve spooned hot over the orange pancakes.

Please note the "Reform" suggestion made below, should you be on a calorie attack at this time.

SENSE ADVANTAGE is just wonderful—soft textures with contrasting sharp fruit taste mellowed by sweetness, and full creamy yet tart finish —and no alcohol needed!

NUTRITION COMMENT relates to the need to understand how to modify to suit specific needs. The recipe given above has a food value, per serving (2 crepes and ¼ of sauce) of:

Crepes	182 calories	8 g. protein	5 g. fat
Sauce	121 calories	1.4 g. protein	7 g. fat
Total	303 calories	9.4 g. protein	12 g. fat

REFORM can be achieved simply by serving one pancake per head and reducing the sauce accordingly by halving the whole recipe. The result is then 152 calories, 4.7 g. protein and 6 g. fat.

Further work can be done by taking out the milk products and substituting non-fat dried milk for the whole milk (see page 169 for milk and below for yoghurt). This would reduce the calories by a further 16 per serving, to 136. You can now compare this to a slice of Angel Food Cake at 135 calories and be convinced (by me) that you will have more of a *mouthful of flavor* from the crepes.

YOGHURT made at home is just super!

Yoghurt has had a pretty good run in nutrition circles, and the commercial boys have leapt on the bandwagon and given it a liberal lacing of sugared fruit pulps to pretty well neutralize the benefits; but it tastes good, doesn't it!

Well, what about one's own yoghurt—how can it be done and what is the cost?

There are two basic procedures. The first uses a Salton system that costs about $12 and leaves nothing to chance.* The other is immediately available to you.

HOMEMADE YOGHURT

Purchase the smallest-size plain, natural yoghurt from your market (or purchase a package of dry starter from a health food store for $2*) and combine one tablespoon with 1 quart milk that has been heated to 100° F. (You can use "2 percent" skim milk for only 125 calories per 8 ounces.) Stir well, put in a glass bowl or 4 8-ounce preserving jars, cover with cloth or lids, and put into an oven preheated to 200° F. Turn oven *off* immediately and leave overnight or about 10 hours. Remove, place in refrigerator and use as required. Suggest adding fresh fruit with a very little honey and wheat germ for sweetness and texture. Always keep one tablespoon of plain yoghurt as a starter for the next batch. It will be necessary to start a new culture every 4 to 6 months, because the yoghurt gets stronger and more acidic with time.

NUTRITIONAL ADVANTAGE can be obtained by using non-fat dried milk in lieu of whole milk. The nourishment obtained in one cup of

* Price at time of writing.

regular yoghurt is the same as for one cup of whole milk. It is a complete protein and provides high amounts of calcium and riboflavin.

EFFORT ADVANTAGE comes from there being almost no effort at all! The use of smaller containers, 1-cup size, is due to the fact that a large quantity, when disturbed, tends to separate and look unsightly.

SENSE ADVANTAGE results in a slight effort expenditure being rewarded with your very own uniquely flavored yoghurt.

YOGHURT DESSERT

Combine 1 cup of low-fat yoghurt with 1 tablespoon sour cream and 4 ounces fresh chopped fruit. Scatter with 1 tablespoon sliced almonds and stir together. Makes a great dessert for 2.

💲 *FRESH PINEAPPLE—the "exotic" fruit that can be decorative*

When pineapples are plentiful, it's a good idea to make the most of the purchase and remove the flesh in such a way that the husk becomes a serving piece. You can make a dessert pineapple, with, say, yoghurt on the side, into a serving visually larger than it really is.

A good pineapple is yellow-green in appearance, especially about the base. Beware of the golden yellow color—it may have gone too far. Another test is to pluck out a center leaf from the top and bend it. It should bend right back without cracking.

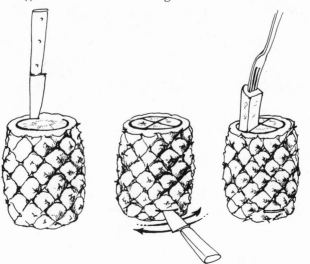

NUTRITIONAL ADVANTAGE. Here you can see the relative effect that processing has upon the foods we eat. A 3½-ounce piece gives us a little over one-third the recommended daily allowance of Vitamin C.

	GRAMS	CALORIES	PROTEIN	FAT	CARBOHY-DRATE
Fresh	100	123	.9 g.	.5 g.	32.3 g.
Canned in Heavy Syrup	100	336	1.4 g.	.5 g.	88 g.

	CALCIUM	IRON	VITAMIN A	VITAMIN C
Fresh	40 mg.	1.2 mg.	170 I.U.	40 mg.
Canned in Heavy Syrup	50 mg.	1.4 mg.	200 I.U.	30 mg.

PINEAPPLE DESSERT

Combine the diced flesh with 1 cup of plain low-fat yoghurt mixed with ¼ cup sour cream and 4 tablespoons of wheat germ. Stir all together well and serve from the chilled husk.

CHOCOLATE SAUCE can have a small place on your menu

Highly appealing this dessert—providing it doesn't run away with you!

CHOCOLATE SAUCE

To melt chocolate place the squares in a small saucepan and cover them with some hot water that is almost at the boil. Use semi-sweet cooking chocolate for best results. Allow to sit in the water on a cold stove, until the chocolate is softened (about 1 to 2 minutes).

Pour off the water gently. To produce a high gloss, add 1½ teaspoons butter to 2 ounces chocolate for a topping suitable for 4 servings. NUTRITION COMMENT. *Be aware of the source of calories.* You can only widen your net to include all the goodies when you know *exactly* what you are eating! Just remember that *ignorance can show!* This sauce has 86 calories per serving, it is delicious and fun to eat but it doesn't take much extra to double the impact to:

1 tablespoon butter + 4 ounces chocolate

and you get *hit* with 172 calories and that is when it gets out of hand!

PEAR HELENE
(*Serves 4*)

2 medium pears	*2 oz. semi-sweet chocolate*
¼ cup dark brown sugar	*1½ tsp. butter*
1 tsp. vanilla	*¾ pt. (1½ cups) vanilla ice cream*

Peel and halve pears; do not remove cores. Dissolve sugar in 2 cups water in skillet. Add vanilla. Place pears in syrup and poach gently until just cooked. Remove pears, scoop out seeds and core. Cover pears with syrup and allow to cool.

Make chocolate sauce as directed above. Beat until smooth and glossy. Place scoop of ice cream in dish, cover with pear half and chocolate sauce.

Beverages

☺ *TEA—the beautiful "herbal" beverage*

The making of tea could hardly be described as an earth-shattering moment, yet so many errors take place that it is quite possibly our worst kitchen moment. Here are some pointers:

- Tea is a fragrant herb—*the bag is insufficient protection.* Keep loose or bagged tea in jars with tightly fitting lids.
- Water should be allowed to run cold to remove the "pipe tastes" before adding to the kettle. This is especially important on Mondays when you may have been away from home and the chlorine has had time to "work" on the pipes and become concentrated.
- Water must boil *freshly;* if it boils too long it reduces the oxygen content that helps to release the aroma.
- "Instant Hot" systems do not make a good cup of tea because the water is heated constantly.
- The kettle should have a flat heavy base for electric and flat top stoves and a large open top to permit easy cleaning. It should be "Teflon" if possible to prevent an aluminum flavor and pot discoloration. Just look inside an old alloy kettle and you will see what I mean!
- For the teapot, clear glass is best because it removes the steeping-time guesswork; you can *see* that it's the right color for you.
- Preheat the teapot by pouring in boiling water; pour it out, add teabags, pour on the *just* boiling water, stir 5 times and leave for 5 minutes.
- Serve China tea with lemon. For other teas, you can have cream,

216

which is added to the cup *after* the tea, otherwise the tea "cracks" the cream, giving an off taste; or milk, which is added to the cup before the tea; or lemon, if you prefer. We use 2% fat milk in preference to the regular.

When using tea bags in a pot, we suggest you detach the swing tags before making. They look ugly hanging out of the pot and also they can impart a paper taste to the tea if left *inside*.

BUDGET CONSIDERATIONS can be important due to the *tea bag count*. This is the number packaged per pound and gives you a clue on the strength you can expect. We buy Red Rose Tea because it has 160 bags to the pound instead of the usual 200. We find that our family gets enough tea for 2 cups each (8 total cups) from only 2 teabags.

SENSE ADVANTAGE is almost entirely aromatic with some taste pluses. The vital thing to remember with tea is to regard it as a fragrant herb and treat it accordingly, for that is what it is!

P.S. We use leftover tea as iced tea, simply pouring the dregs into an old ½-gallon fruit juice jar with a screw cap.

NEW WINE RECIPES

We used, for our tests, Welch's White and Red Grape Juices. These are bottled pure grape juices and do not need reconstitution.

We are sure that there must be many other companies that process what we call new wine (non-alcoholic grape juice), but we are equally certain that the degree of natural sweetness will differ in each case; therefore we use this name only as a base for our recipe measurements and not as an endorsement of its superior qualities.

NEW WHITE COOKING WINE

This can be used in place of dry white wine called for in recipe books.

½ cup (4 fl. oz.) white grape juice   1 tsp. rice vinegar

Combine and use immediately.

NEW RED COOKING WINE

Use in lieu of red wines called for in recipe books.

½ cup (4 fl. oz.) red (or purple)   1 tbsp. strong cold tea
   grape juice   1 tbsp. rice vinegar

Combine and use immediately.

You will find that I separate the grape juice and tea from the vinegar in some recipes for specific effects.

ST. VINCENTS WINE CUP

¾ cup (6 fl. oz.) white grape juice   2 leaves fresh mint
1 tbsp. "Rose's lime juice"

Makes 2 4-ounce wine glasses for 13¢ a glass. Serve chilled on the rocks with mint as garnish.

NEW APPLE WINE

⅝ cup (5 fl. oz.) white grape   ¼ cup (2 fl. oz.) clear apple juice
   juice   1 cup ice cubes

Combine items at slow speed in a blender. Serve garnished with a slice of red apple, coated with lemon juice to prevent browning—and a straw. Makes 2 cups (16 fluid ounces) of juice at 24 calories per 4-ounce wine glass.

NEW CLARET

1 bottle (24 fl. oz) red grape juice   ¼–½ cup (2–4 fl. oz.) strong cold
                                                tea—add gradually to taste

Make tea by pouring ¾ cup (6 fl. oz.) *boiling* water onto a teabag. Press it thoroughly and let it steep until cold. Remove the teabag and add the cold tea to the grape juice.

Serve *lightly* chilled. It has an interesting turn in flavor associated with some claret wines.

NEW SANGRIA

Use New Claret recipe (above), but add 1 orange and 1 lemon, both finely sliced, and 1 teaspoon Angustura Bitters. Add ice and serve.

General Miscellany

🙂 *OMELET PAN cured of rust and sticking*

It is quite easy nowadays to buy a generally low cost pan made of steel or cast iron with an attached handle of the same material. They are heavy, spread the heat well and they rust. The handles also get dangerously hot.

We advise buying an omelet/crepe pan 7 inches in diameter, of plain iron metal. This type is seldom, if ever, washed. Washing creates moisture and moisture means rust whereas constant absorption of fat means a non-stick finish.

In order to prepare such a pan for use, you must "cure" it with 1 cup inexpensive cooking oil. First *wash the pan* in plenty of boiling hot soapy water and rinse thoroughly; *place it wet* on the stove to dry. When completely dry, add 2 tablespoons (⅛ cup) oil and leave at medium high for 5 minutes. Add enough salt to absorb all the oil and rub it into the pan with paper towels or newspaper. Repeat this action 8 times until all the oil has been used. Then lightly oil the pan all over and use when you need it, cleaning with oil and salt after each use.

💰 *PORTABLE TIMERS keep you out of trouble*

Each kitchen is equipped with a clock—it's on your wrist, on the wall or built into the oven. Some of these can be made to remind you of things by buzzing. But I am unable to relax and enjoy my kitchen unless I have a buzzer literally on my person!

220

I purchased a two-hour (Swiss movement) "parking ticket" timer for about $6 and it turned out to be a gold mine of relief. No matter where I wander over the house, in the study, or on the phone, its little relentless self is ticking away, keeping an eye on those fragile foods that can be ruined by overcooking. Clearly I'd recommend it to anyone who likes to be relaxed in his/her kitchen and not have that perpetual fear of forgetting something.

KNIVES *supersharp with ease*

Well-sharpened knives are a joy to use and, surprisingly, inflict fewer wounds. They are certainly more efficient when slicing and could conceivably contribute to some savings as a result, especially with the carving knife.

Here is the method I like best—it provides complete control and safety even to the absolute beginner.

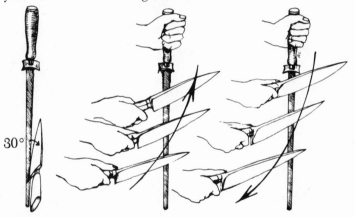

KNIFE AT 30° ANGLE	UPWARD SWING	DOWNWARD SWING
SHARPEN ONE SIDE	TO POSITION	TO SHARPEN
THEN THE OTHER		

SUPERMARKET *chart of dangerous reefs!*

This is the layout I shared with you on television.

Briefly the idea is that a supermarket should be viewed as a coral atoll surrounded by uncharted reefs. The object is to get in, shop and get out *without running aground!*

By this, I mean we need to know where to go to get what, and we need to know exactly what we need before we get into the front door! This is why I use this chart.

You will note that I made 17 stops for the things I knew I needed. I came out a whole man. I was not tempted by "specials" that I had not already read about and planned to shop for *on the form*. I stuck to the track laid out and wasn't "inspired" once. That is the *only* way I can shop and save and it took us about 2 hours to draw up the chart and run off a few copies. Please try it.

So now it is ended, and the last words are to be written.

May the Grace of God, the example of our Lord and Savior Jesus Christ and the infilling of the Holy Spirit be with you all the days of your life.

Amen.

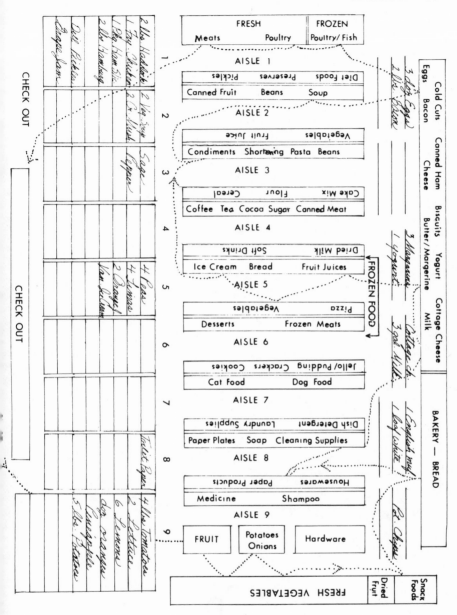

Index